ON STAGE!

Women in Landscape_Architecture and Planning

Hg./Eds.: Barbara Zibell | Doris Damyanovic | Eva Álvarez

ON STAGE!

Women in Landscape_Architecture and Planning

jovis

Impressum

WEITER_DENKEN is a series by **ist eine Reihe des**
Forum für GenderKompetenz in Architektur Landschaft Planung
(gender_archland)
Fakultät für Architektur und Landschaft
Leibniz Universität Hannover
© 2016 by jovis Verlag GmbH

Cover Umschlag
BOKU; text Text: Martina Jauschneg

Editors Herausgeberinnen
Barbara Zibell, Doris Damyanovic, Eva Álvarez

Editors Assistance Redaktionsassistenz
Kirsten Aleth, Aurélie Karlinger

Editing Lektorat
Ursula Liebl, Maria Lücking, Aurélie Karlinger

Design and setting Gestaltung und Satz
Aurélie Karlinger, Anjoulie Brandner, Hannah K. Jenal, Eva Álvarez, Verena Beiser, Florian Reinwald

Printing and binding Druck und Bindung
DZS Grafik, d. o. o., Ljubljana

Bibliographic information published by the Deutsche Nationalbibliothek
The Deutsche Nationalbibliothek lists this publication in the Deutsche Nationalbibliografie;
detailed bibliographic data are available on the Internet at http://dnb.d-nb.de

Bibliografische Information der Deutschen Nationalbibliothek
Die Deutsche Nationalbibliothek verzeichnet diese Publikation in der Deutschen National-
bibliografie; detaillierte bibliografische Daten sind im Internet über http://dnb.d-nb.de abrufbar.

jovis Verlag GmbH
Kurfürstenstraße 15/16
10785 Berlin
www.jovis.de

jovis books are available worldwide in select bookstores. Please contact your nearest bookseller
or visit www.jovis.de for information concerning your local distribution.

jovis-Bücher sind weltweit im ausgewählten Buchhandel erhältlich. Informationen zu unserem
internationalen Vertrieb erhalten Sie von Ihrem Buchhändler oder unter www.jovis.de.

ISBN 978-3-86859-466-9

Inhaltsverzeichnis Table of Content

Einleitung

Barbara Zibell, Doris Damyanovic, Eva Álvarez

On Stage x 3! Women in Landscape_Architecture and Planning

On Stage! ist ein internationales Projekt der Frauen- und Geschlechterforschung, das darauf abzielt, Frauen im Bereich der planenden und bauenden Disziplinen sichtbar zu machen. Seit mehr als 100 Jahren haben sie Zugang zu Hochschulen und Universitäten und arbeiten als Architektinnen, so wie Männer dies tun, seit der Beruf des Architekten geschaffen wurde. Nichtsdestotrotz werden Fachfrauen bis heute vielfach eher als Sekretärinnen oder Assistentinnen gesehen denn als Teil des kreativen Stabs. „Wo sind die Frauen in der Architektur?" – so lautet auch der Titel eines Buches und die Frage, die kürzlich von der US-amerikanischen Wissenschaftlerin Despina Stratigakos (2016) aufgeworfen wurde, mit der sie die Realitäten betreffend Gleichstellung der Geschlechter in diesem Berufsfeld bestätigt. Nicht nur in der Praxis, auch in Forschung und Lehre sind Frauen bis heute stets unterrepräsentiert. Sie fehlen in historischen Betrachtungen ebenso wie auf Universitätsprofessuren und als Forschungsgegenstand.

On Stage! wollte und will Frauen in den planenden und gestaltenden Disziplinen sichtbar machen – nicht nur als ausgezeichnete, und bezogen auf ihr Oeuvre international bekannte Architektinnen, sondern auch in ihren familiären und persönlichen Kontexten. Das Projekt zielt darauf ab, einen Einblick in das Zusammenspiel des beruflichen wie alltäglichen Lebens von Frauen zu zeigen und verständlich zu machen.

Die „dreifache" Ausstellung, die in diesem Band dokumentiert ist, wurde bisher in drei verschiedenen europäischen Städten gezeigt: in Hannover 2011, in Valencia 2012 und zweimal in Wien 2014. Mit den Ausstellungen in Wien erweiterte sich auch das Spektrum der porträtierten Frauen vom engeren Fokus der Architektur und Landschaftsarchitektur auf weitere Disziplinen der Landschafts-, Raum- und Umweltplanung.

Ausgangspunkt der Ausstellung

Diese Ausstellung ist nicht einfach eine Wanderausstellung, wie man sie weltweit kennt. Es ist vielmehr eine fortschreitende, wachsende Ausstellung, die sich von Ort zu Ort verändert, abhängig von den Akteurinnen und Akteuren der involvierten Universitäten – Studierenden wie Lehrenden, die jeweils daran arbeiten.

Die Idee für diese Fortsetzungsausstellung entstand am Forum für Gender Kompetenz in Architektur Landschaft Planung (gender_archland) an der Fakultät für Architektur und Landschaft, Leibniz Universität Hannover (LUH), und wurde erstmalig zusammen mit der Architektenkammer Niedersachsen gezeigt. Nicht weniger als drei Bedingungen machten diese Ausstellung möglich:
1. Die Idee – inspiriert von „La Mujer construye", einer Ausstellung über Architektinnen in Spanien, die seit 1999 mehrere Länder – wie Italien, Niederlande und Libanon – bereist hat.
2. Die Initiatorin – die erste Gastprofessorin am gender_archland, Lidewij Tummers von der Technischen Universität Delft (TU Delft), die das Ausstellungsprojekt kannte und es nach Hannover holen, mit Studierenden weiterentwickeln und in den deutschen akademischen Kontext einführen wollte.
3. Die Verfügbarkeit von (Landschafts-)Architektinnen in der Region Hannover, die bereit waren, sich auf ein solch zeit- und ressourcenverzehrendes Experiment mit offenem Ausgang einzulassen.
Aus dem Dreiklang entstand unter der Bezeichnung „A Different Way to Practise?" im Sommersemester

Introduction

Barbara Zibell, Doris Damyanovic, Eva Álvarez

On Stage x 3! Women in Landscape Architecture and Planning

On Stage! is an international women's and gender studies project which aims at making female architects and planning experts visible. For more than 100 years, women have been able to study and work as architects in the same way as men, since the profession of architect had been established. Nonetheless, female experts are still often perceived as assistants or secretaries to their male colleagues and not considered as part of the creative staff in offices – especially in architecture. 'Where are the Women Architects?' was a question raised by a young American expert on women in architecture who attested the sad stateof gender equality in the architectural profession today (Stratigakos 2016: 21ff). Not only in practice, but also in teaching and research, women as professionals have always been and still are underrepresented. They are absent from historical consideration among university professors and topics of research.

On Stage! wanted and wants to make women visible as professionals – not only for being excellent and internationally known architects in regard to their 'œuvre', but also in their personal and family contexts. It aims at showing and making understandable the everyday life in which the professional activity of women architects are embedded. Until now, this 'threefold' exhibition has taken place among three different places in Europe: in Hanover 2011, in Valencia 2012 and twice in Vienna 2014. The exhibitions in Vienna have also expanded the range of women portrayed, from the narrower focus of architecture and landscape architecture to other disciplines of landscape, spatial and environmental planning.

The exhibition's starting point

On Stage! is not only a travelling, continuous exhibition, familiar by other exhibitions of the same kind from around the world. It is, beyond, a developing exhibition which is growing and changing from place to place. The idea was born at the Forum for Gender Competence in Architecture Landscape Planning (gender_archland), Faculty of Architecture and Landscape Sciences, at Leibniz Universität Hannover (LUH) and performed for the first time in cooperation with the Chamber of Architects in Lower Saxony. Not less than three pre-conditions made its existence possible:

1. The idea – derived from 'La Mujer construye', an exhibition on women architects in Spain, that travelled several countries – as far as Italy, the Netherlands and Lebanon – since 1999
2. The promoter – the first female guest professor at gender_archland, Lidewij Tummers from the Technical University of Delft (TU Delft) – was familiar with this exhibition and wanted to bring it to Hanover in Germany and develop it with students among a German academic context
3. The availability of female (landscape) architects in the region of Hanover ready to engage in such an open-end, time- and resource-consuming experiment.

Out of these three conditions and with the title 'A different way to practise', a student project was developed during the summer term of 2010 and got published in an e-volume within the gender_archland series ('WEITER_DENKEN' 2). For various reasons – primarily lack of funds – the idea of taking the international exhibition from Madrid to Hanover was not feasible.

9

2010 ein Projekt mit Studierenden, das mit dem Ablauf der Gastprofessur von Lidewij Tummers endete und als Band 2 in der Schriftenreihe des gender_archland („WEITER_DENKEN" 2) publiziert wurde (TUMMERS und NIESCKEN, 2010).

Verschiedene Gründe – vor allem der Mangel an finanziellen Mitteln – führten dazu, dass die Idee, diese internationale Ausstellung von Madrid nach Hannover zu holen, nicht umgesetzt werden konnte.

On Stage! Hannover, Stop 2011

Und so unternahm die zweite Gastprofessorin am gender_archland, Eva Álvarez von der Universitat Politècnica de València (UPV), im Wintersemester 2010/11 einen neuen Anlauf mit einer neuen Gruppe von Studierenden, um ein Ausstellungsprojekt über Architektinnen, deren Leben und deren Werk, „auf die Bühne" zu bringen – der Titel „On Stage!" war geboren. Hauptbezugspunkt in diesem Kontext war der Text von Denise Scott Brown „Sexism and the Star System in Architecture" (1989/2009), in dem sie ihre eigenen Erfahrungen als Büropartnerin und Frau eines berühmten Architekten zu Papier bringt und beschreibt, wie sie stets in die zweite Reihe, auf die Rolle der Sekretärin, verwiesen wurde.

Aus dieser Perspektive, dem Blickwinkel der Architektinnen mit ihren vielfältigen und komplexen Rahmenbedingungen aus professioneller Erwerbsarbeit und unbezahlter Hausarbeit, Privatheit und öffentlichem Auftritt entwickelten die Studierenden zusammen mit ihrer Dozentin die Inhalte zur Ausstellung – nah am Material der sieben deutschen bzw. niedersächsischen Architektinnen, die aus der ersten Runde noch dabei waren, zzgl. weiterer sieben ausgewählter Architektinnen aus anderen Ländern der Welt, zu denen „unsere" Studierenden, selbst von unterschiedlichster Herkunft, eine besondere Beziehung hatten. Aus dieser Arbeit, die sich über ein einziges Semester erstreckte, entstand das, was als erste Ausstellung unter dem Titel On Stage! in Hannover 2011 gezeigt wurde. Ergebnis der Zusammenarbeit zwischen Studierenden der Architektur und der Landschaftsarchitektur, zwischen Hannover und Valencia, in einem intensiven und zielstrebigen Prozess, der letztendlich nicht nur Ausstellungstafeln hervorbrachte, sondern auch Timeline, Flyer (in Form einer Brille als Symbol für den anderen Blick), Audio Guide (in Deutsch, Englisch, Spanisch) und temporär eingerichtete Website. Die Ausstellung, erstmals zu sehen im repräsentativen Laveshaus der Architektenkammer Niedersachsen in Hannover, wurde mit einer festlichen Vernissage eröffnet und mit einer Diskussionsrunde zwischen Architektinnen und Studentinnen im Rahmen einer Finissage beendet. Einige Monate später „wanderte" die Ausstellung erstmalig an einen anderen Ort, noch in Hannover: zur Fakultät für Architektur und Landschaft der Leibniz Universität. Der Festvortrag wurde von einer der in der Ausstellung porträtierten Architektinnen, Sheila Sri Prakash aus Chennai, Indien, gehalten.

Während dieser Zeit, im Sommersemester 2011, war bereits eine dritte Gastwissenschaftlerin, Doris Damyanovic vom Institut für Landschaftsplanung an der Universität für Bodenkultur Wien (BOKU Wien), am gender_archland tätig. Im Kontext ihrer Lehre und zur Vorbereitung einer weiteren Ausgabe der Ausstellung On Stage! in Spanien unternahm sie, gemeinsam mit Barbara Zibell und Studierenden der Architektur und Landschaftsarchitektur, unter dem Titel „Analyse der Alltagsqualitäten urbaner Räume" eine Exkursion nach Barcelona und Valencia.

On Stage! Valencia, Stop 2012

Die Ausstellung On Stage! wurde gestaltet, um auf Reisen zu gehen und neue Inhalte und Ausstellungstafeln zu entwickeln, solange Nachfrage da war. Das machte es möglich, die aktuellen Themen "OUT THERE, RIGHT NOW" (DORT DRAUSSEN, GERADE JETZT) zu verfolgen. Dabei war die Herausforderung, die Arbeit von Architektinnen mit aktuellen Medien darzustellen und neue Perspektiven auf das Werk von Frauen zu legen. Dabei ist hervorzuheben, wie schwierig es ist, den gegenwärtigen Zustand des Berufs für Frauen (und Männer) zu präsentieren. Infolgedessen musste das Material im Zuge der

On Stage! Hanover, Stop 2011

The second female gender_archland guest professor, Eva Álvarez from the Universitat Politècnica de València (UPV), made a fresh attempt with a new group of students during the winter term of 2010/11 by bringing an exhibition project on women architects to 'the stage'. The title 'On Stage!' was born. For her teaching activities in this context, the main reference she used was the star system in architecture, described by Denise Scott Brown in 1989 'Sexism and the Star System in Architecture', a paper in which the named author presented her own experiences as partner and wife of a famous architect, describing her situation as always being relegated to second rank, and role of assistant (SCOTT BROWN, 1989/2009).

Out of this perspective of female architects and a focus on their varying life situations – considering determining factors as professional and paid work, home and unpaid work, privacy and publicity – the students developed the content of the exhibition in cooperation with and support by their teacher, using previously elaborated material from seven female architects from Lower Saxony, Germany who had participated in the project in the very beginning. Thereafter another seven female architects from all around the world were selected by the students' own specific interest. This work which lasted a single term, culminated in the first On Stage! exhibition in Hanover, representing the outcome of an international cooperation between students of architecture and landscape architecture, between Hanover and Valencia, in an intensive and systematic process involving the creation of panels, a timeline, a flyer in the shape of a pair of glasses (symbolising a 'different' perspective), an audio guide (in German, English and Spanish), and a temporary website. The exhibition, held in the prestigious Laveshaus building of the Chamber of Architects in Lower Saxony was inaugurated with an informal preview and closed by a public discussion between the students and some of the female architects portrayed in the exhibition. For the first time, some months later, the exhibition travelled to a different place within Hanover: to the Faculty of Architecture and Landscape Sciences, Leibniz Universität Hannover. There, the keynote lecture was held by one of the international female specialists featured in the exhibition, architect Sheila Sri Prakash from Chennai, India.

Since then, during the summer term of 2011, a third guest researcher joined gender_archland: Doris Damyanovic of the Institute of Landscape Planning, University of Natural Resources and Life Sciences (BOKU Vienna), Vienna. Within the context of her teaching and in the framework of the preparation for the next exhibition phase of On Stage! under the title 'Analysing Daily Life Qualities in Urban Spaces' she undertook an excursion to Barcelona and Valencia together with some of her architecture and landscape students.

On Stage! Valencia, Stop 2012

The On Stage! exhibition was designed as a mobile exhibition to travel and to develop new material for as long as there was demand for it. This made it possible to assess the current issues OUT THERE, RIGHT NOW, as we noticed how difficult it is to show female architects' work using current media and how even more difficult it is to show a new perspective on women's work – without mentioning the difficulties to outline the present state of the profession for women.

Once the exhibition in Hanover was over, it was transported to Valencia, where new original material by architects and Master students from the School of Architecture at UPV was added. The initial – and final – aims were to investigate, show and assess female architects' work from a gender perspective. In pursuing this aspiration, a students' work seminar was conducted during March, April and May 2012, to which Doris Damyanovic and Barbara Zibell were also invited to teach, in order to decide how women's work should be displayed. We also invited selected women architects to the seminar, with the intention of including some of their ideas to the design and production of the new material to be exhibited in Valencia.

Recherchen, wo auch immer die Ausstellung gerade stattfand, immer wieder neu hervorgebracht werden.

Sobald die Ausstellung in Hannover zu Ende war, wurden die Ausstellungstafeln nach Valencia transportiert, wo diesen originäres Material von ArchitektInnen und Masterstudierenden an der Architekturfakultät der UPV, Spanien, hinzugefügt wurde. Ziel war, das Werk von Architektinnen zu recherchieren, zu dokumentieren und aus einer Genderperspektive zu bewerten. Um dieses Ziel zu erreichen, fand im März, April und Mai 2012 ein Seminar mit Studierenden statt, zu dem auch Doris Damyanovic und Barbara Zibell eingeladen wurden. Die Ausstellung in Valencia wurde in Form von Lebenslinien, persönlichen Interviews und Videoaufnahmen präsentiert.

On Stage! Wien, Stop 2014

Die Umsetzung in Wien 2014 erfolgte durch die Kooperation von Studierenden und Lehrenden der Universität für Bodenkultur Wien (BOKU Wien), geleitet von Doris Damyanovic und der Technischen Universität Wien (TU Wien), geleitet von Gesa Witthöft und Petra Hirschler. Im Rahmen des Seminars „Gender and Diversity Aspects in Planning and Practice", angeboten an beiden Universitäten im Wintersemester 2013/14, wurde das Konzept für On Stage! Vienna 2014 entwickelt. Zehn Studierende hatten elf Expertinnen aus Politik und Verwaltung, Hochschulen und Planungsbüros zu feministischer und genderspezifischer Planung interviewt.

Die Ausstellung zeigt den Werdegang der Frauen und eine Auswahl ihrer gender-sensiblen Projekte. Die Inhalte wurden in Form von Postern, Projekt-Würfeln, Timeline, Podium und «Freecards» mit Zitaten umgesetzt, begleitet durch Gastbeiträge von Eva Álvarez und Barbara Zibell begleitet. Die Ausstellung fand vom 27. März bis 24. April 2014 in der Hauptbibliothek der BOKU Wien statt. Etwa 80 Personen kamen zur Vernissage, die von einer Tanzperformance begleitet wurde. Die Timeline ist mittlerweile in der Bibliothek als permanente Installation aufgestellt. Im Sommersemester wurde das Seminar an der TU Wien ein zweites Mal angeboten. Geleitet von Gesa Witthöft und Petra Hirschler von der TU Wien erarbeiteten die Studierenden ein Ausstellungskonzept als Teil der internationalen European Gender Equality Conference im September 2014. Alle drei Ausstellungen wurden gemeinsam als Rahmenprogramm zur Konferenz gezeigt.

Dokumentation – ohne Fortsetzung?

Der vorliegende Band dokumentiert die Ausstellung an den drei genannten Standorten und kommentiert am Ende den Stand der Dinge, ohne das Vorhaben als ein abgeschlossenes Projekt zu betrachten. So wie es anfing, soll es auch weitergehen – und wir wünschen uns, dass diesem Anfang weitere Ausstellungen an anderen Orten in Europa und rund um den Erdball folgen werden.

Das Projekt zielt darauf ab, fortgesetzt zu werden und will Vernetzung erreichen sowie nicht zuletzt die Transformation der Geschlechterverhältnisse im Sinne von Chancengleichheit im Beruf und gerechter Aufteilung von bezahlter und unbezahlter Arbeit zwischen den Geschlechtern.

Wir wünschen allen Leserinnen und Lesern eine bereichernde Lektüre und Betrachtung und hoffen, dass der Beitrag der porträtierten Frauen zur Planung und Gestaltung unserer gemeinsamen Umwelt stellvertretend für alle (noch) nicht porträtierten Vertreterinnen aller planenden und gestaltenden Disziplinen nach und nach eine höhere Wertschätzung erfahren möge.

Elements created for the exhibition in Valencia revealed great potential to introduce this approach. This precise idea was intended to be visualized by intertwined timelines and personal interviews, some of them video recorded.

On Stage! Vienna, Stop 2014

The realisation of On Stage! Vienna 2014 was achieved through the cooperation of students and teachers of the BOKU Vienna with Doris Damyanovic and the University of Technology Vienna (TU Vienna) with Gesa Witthöft and Petra Hirschler. In the context of a seminar entitled 'Gender and Diversity Aspects in Planning and Practice' – offered at both universities during the winter term of 2013/14 – the concept for On Stage! Vienna 2014 was developed.

Ten students interviewed eleven experts from politics, administration, universities and planning offices, in the sphere of feminist and gender-specific planning. The exhibition showed their development and select gender-sensitive projects. The contents were communicated through posters, project-profile cubes, a timeline, a podium and free cards with quotations from the experts.

The development and implementation of the project were supported by guest contributions from Eva Álvarez and Prof. Barbara Zibell. The exhibition took place between 27 March and 24 April 2014 in the main library of BOKU Vienna. Around 80 people attended the opening, accompanied by dance performance. The timeline is now a permanent installation in the library hall.

During the summer term of 2014 the seminar was again proposed at the TU Vienna with Gesa Witthöft and Petra Hirschler. The students developed a framework programme for the 8th European Conference of Gender Equality in Higher Education in September 2014. All three exhibitions were shown together.

Documentation – with(out) continuation?

This volume documents the exhibition at the three aforementioned locations and comments the status quo of the closing, without considering the venture to be a completed project. It should continue as it started – we hope that more exhibitions will follow this beginning in more places in Europe and around the world. The project wants to go further and beyond, to form a network and transform gender relations around the world with the objective of having equal conditions of professionalism in architecture and planning based on equal division of labour between women and men. We therefore hope that all readers will find this publication to be an enriching read, and that it will encourage further reflection. We hope too that the contribution of the women portrayed, to planning and designing the world we share will be widely appreciated as they speak for all planning and design disciplines not (yet) portrayed.

REFERENCES

SCOTT BROWN, Denise (1989/2009): Sexism and the Star System in Architecture, in: Having Words, London: Architectural Association Publications, 2009: 79–89. Originally published as 'Room at the Top? Sexism and the Star System in Architecture,' in Architecture: A Place for Women, ed. Ellen Perry Berkeley and Matilda McQuaid, Washington, DC: Smithsonian Institution Press, 1989: 237–46.

STRATIGAKOS, Despina (2016): Where Are the Women Architects?. Princeton University Press. New Jersey.

TUMMERS, Lidewij; NIESCKEN, Johanna (2011): A Different Way to Practice? Deutsche (Landschafts-) Architektinnen im internationalen Vergleich – A Transdiciplinary Project (weiter denken, 2). Hannover, www.gender-archland.uni-hannover.de/fileadmin/gender-archland/Dokumente/weiter_denken2.pdf (access on 13.09.2016).

2009|2010

First female guest professor Lidewij Tummers (TU Delft) at gender_archland developed a similar concept with German students at LUH in the context to the Spanish idea. The output was the e-publication 'A different way to practise'. Primarily due to a lack of funds, the Spainish exhibition could not be shown in Hanover.

© gender_archland

since 1999

'La Mujer construye' an exhibition on women architects in Spain that travelled several countries e.g. Italy, Netherlands and Lebanon

Winter term 2010_11 – The second female guest professor Eva Álvarez (UPV) set a new start with a group of students from architecture and landscape architecture. The idea of On Stage! was born.

March 2010 – The first exhibition with 7 female architects from Lower Saxony and 7 from all over the world was shown in in the Laveshaus in Hanover.

Summer term 2011 – The third guest professor Doris Damyanovic (BOKU Vienna) together with Barbara Zibell (LUH) and Eva Álvarez (UPV) further developed the idea of On Stage! as a collaborative teaching and research project. An excursion with students to Valencia and Barcelona was organised by Zibell and Damyanovic.

November 2011 – The exhibition was shown at the LUH. The keynote lecture was held by one of the portrayed women: architect Sheila Sri Prakash from Chennai, India.

© LUH

© LUH

On Stage! Valencia, Stop	On Stage! Vienna, Stop	Vienna Mélange!
2012	**2014**	**2014**

ON STAGE

Summer term 2012 – The Hanover exhibition was transported to Valencia. During a student project the next exhibitions were prepared. Also Barbara Zibell and Doris Damyanovic contributed to this seminar.

Mai 2012 – The Hanover exhibition which was extended by 7 female architects from Spain, Argentina and Brazil. It was shown at UPV.

Winter term 2013_2014 – The concept for On Stage! Vienna was developed during the seminar offered at the BOKU Vienna from Doris Damyanovic and TU Vienna, Gesa Witthöft and Petra Hirschler. Eva Álvarez shared her experiences with the ten students during the seminar.

March 2014 – Vernissage of On Stage! Vienna at the library hall at the BOKU. 11 female experts in the field of gender-sensitive planning were shown. Barbara Zibell held the keynote speech.

Summer term 2014 – The next seminar was organised by the TU Vienna. The students prepared a framework programme for the 8th European Conference on Gender Equality in Higher Education.

September 2014 – On Stage! Mélange – On Stage x 3! was shown at the conference. A session on 'Gender Issues in Teaching and Research' was part of the programme.

© Lola Domènech

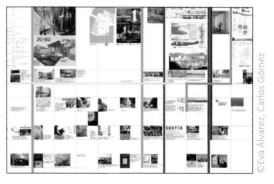

© Eva Álvarez, Carlos Gómez

© BOKU Wien, TU Wien

HANNOVERHANOVER

On Stage! Hanover, Stop 2011

Hannah Jenal, Barbara Zibell

The activities around the exhibition in Hanover were initiated with the essay 'Sexism and the Star System in Architecture' (1989/2008) by Denise Scott Brown, forwarded to the students by guest professor Eva Álvarez. This text, written by a female architect (born in 1931), who, during her life, managed an practice together with her partner, Robert Venturi, developed projects and published theories on architecture which – as many women specialists involved in the exhibition confirm – have not lost any of their relevance until today. In her essay, Denise Scott Brown writes about her experience of being overlooked beside 'him', constantly being pushed into the background and generally being addressed as the secretary and not as a creative architect. This culminated in the fact that in 1991, the prestigious Pritzker Prize, the 'Nobel prize for architecture', was awarded to him only, with disregard of her accomplishments. A petition presented by Denise Scott Brown to the jury some 20 years later was dismissed in 2013.

The number of women taking up architectural studies has continued to rise in recent years. The proportion of female students at the Leibniz Universität Hannover now exceeds 50 %. Nevertheless, women and their contribution to architecture – both in construction and urban planning history as well as in the principles of building design – have been underrepresented up to now although they existed – even before they were admitted to academic study. In Landscape Architecture, in Hanover a course closely associated to Architecture, the ratio is different – here the proportion of female students has traditionally always been higher. Landscape seems to be a 'female' domain. But even here, as with Architecture, the majority of women are not represented in the higher echelons of the academic hierarchy. Women are rarely to be found in the top positions.

Women in (Landscape) Architecture and Planning – where are they, what are they thinking, how do they live and work, in what contexts do they operate, what building and planning tasks are particularly important to them? These were the reasons why, together with interested students, we sought out women in architectural professions for the exhibition project. The 'pioneers' that Kerstin Dörhöfer, a German female theorist in architecture, portrayed (2004), the first female architects in Berlin, continue to write history and created a story that completes the story of men and their architectural works.

REFERENCES

DÖRHÖFER, Kerstin (2004): Pionierinnen in der Architektur. Eine Baugeschichte der Moderne. Tübingen: Ernst Wasmuth Verlag.

SCOTT BROWN, Denise (1989/2009): Sexism and the Star System in Architecture, in: Having Words, London: Architectural Association Publications, 2009: 79–89. Originally published as 'Room at the Top? Sexism and the Star System in Architecture,' in Architecture: A Place for Women, ed. Ellen Perry Berkeley and Matilda McQuaid, Washington, DC: Smithsonian Institution Press, 1989: 237–46.

On Stage! Hanover Stop

Coordinators:
Eva Álvarez and Barbara Zibell, Katja Stock_Leibniz Universität Hannover (LUH),
Ute Maasberg_Chamber of Architects, Lower Saxony (AKNds)

(Landscape) Architects:
National: Katja Ahad, Karin Bukies, Karin Kellner, Barbara Maria Kirsch, Brigitte Nieße, Sabine Rebe, Johanna Sievers

International: Niloufar M. Aliha, Iran, Eva Álvarez, Spain, England, Jannina Cabal, Ecuador, Sheila Sri Prakash, India, Lidewij Tummers, The Netherlands, Maria Viñé and Martina Voser, Switzerland

Students: Berivan Akin, Katharina Bornschein, Claudia Alejandra Falconi Burbano, Ashkan Golfar, Hannah Katharina Jenal, Mohammed Abdessalem Laaribi, Anna Ziegler

Vernissage and finissage organisation:
Ute Maasberg

Vernissage speakers:
Wolfgang Schneider, President AKNds,
Barbara Zibell, Professor, Leibniz Universität Hannove
Eva Álvarez, Guestprofessor, Leibniz Universität Hannover

Finissage speakers: Katja Ahad, Claudia Falconi, Hannah Katharina Jenal, Karin Kellner, Johanna Sievers, Barbara Zibell, Anna Ziegler

Financial support:
City and Region of Hanover (Equal opportunity commissioner), Equal opportunity commissioner and Friends of the LUH, Dr. Marie Helene Fastje Foundation, Licht Jentsch

The exhibition

This exhibition displays 13 architectural practices from across the world and tells the stories of women in charge – their family backgrounds and their career progressions. The chosen examples are meant to encourage and to point out that excelling in one's profession despite prejudices and planning a family is, after all, possible.
We intentionally chose practices that deal with the following topics: sustainability, social and environmental issues, low budget construction and day-to-day problems.
Nowadays, prospective and also practising architects need role models who address values. Another core area displayed today is teamwork.
Most of today's projects are dealt with in groups – individual work is becoming the exception.

To start with, there were seven students, five women and two men, from both courses, Architecture and Landscape Architecture. By the end, only three students remained to complete the project assisted, to some extent, by their male co-students who supported them during the final night shifts. The whole project – from initial concept through to realisation, materialisation, production and creation of the design structure for the Chamber of Architects´Laves House – was created in the context of a student course with 5/6 credit points (30 CP per semester are obligatory), i.e. ultimately with multiple outputs to be expected in such a context. The students' achievement in terms of work and perseverance has been astounding, against all the odds and the constant challenges they faced. They have learnt a great deal, but have also achieved much – for themselves and for the regional and (inter) national specialist community.

Women (and Men) in Landscape Architecture and Planning...

... from Lower Saxony

Katja Ahad	AHAD Architekten
Barbara Maria Kirsch	kirsch architekten
Karin Kellner	KSW Architekten und Stadtplaner
Brigitte Nieße	plan zwei, Stadtplanung und Architektur
Johanna Sievers	SPALINK-SIEVERS Landschaftsarchitekten
Karin Bukies	Stadtlandschaft
Sabine Rebe	wohnplan, architektur und beratung

... and around the world

Eva Maria Álvarez	GOMEZ+ALVAREZ ARQUITECTS, Valencia, Spain
Lidewij Tummers	Tussen Ruimte, Rotterdam, The Netherlands
Maria Viñé and Martina Voser	vi.vo, Zurich, Switzerland
Jannina Cabal	Jannina Cabal Arquitectos, Guayaquil, Ecuador
Niloufar M. Aliha	Part Ham-Goruh Andish, Tehran, Iran
Sheila Sri Prakash	Shilpa ARCHITECTS + PLANNERS + DESIGNERS, Chennai, India

© Jana Fischer

The idea of recycling

The idea of recycling materials is not new, but it fits in with regard to content in various ways and contributes an innovative and refreshing aspect to an at times monotonous appearance of today's architecture. Ultimately, the gender discussion's main purpose is to reduce old clichés. The different materials reflect the practices' diverse approach to various working methods. Sustainability is an important factor in many projects – in both today's working environment and this exhibition. To emphasize this, the panels bearing the exhibition's placards are made of recycled chipboard.

The timeline

The timeline (photographs) is an important part of the exhibition concept. It combines pictures through the decades of all portrayed women about their career. You can see and combine the timeline with the panels how private life influenced their style of planning and designing. It allows you to see 'behind the scenes'.

The audioguide

The exhibition offered the visitor an audioguide to each portrait with original recordings from the interview. It was available in German, English and Spanish.

Location:
Chamber of Architects, Lower Saxony, Germany

© Jana Fischer

© Jana Fischer

Location:
Chamber of Architects, Lower Saxony, Germany

portraits on the exhibition area window
– people did not need to go inside to see the inside

Concept of the exhibition panels

The exhibition was firstly designed for the location
of the Chamber of Architects of Lower Saxony
(Germany).
The location was offered to this project by the
Chamber and was 6 weeks on.

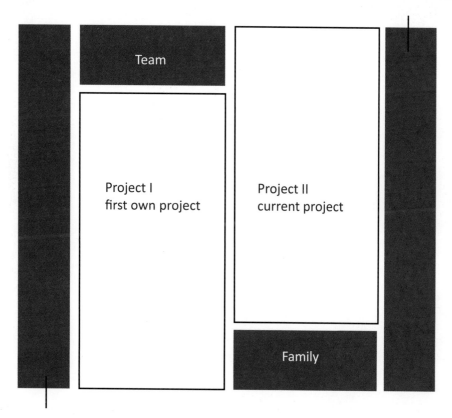

the architect and family

Team

Project I
first own project

Project II
current project

Family

the architect and team

KATJA AHAD
BRUNSWICK, GERMANY

'Architects who have never experienced family life as it should be will always find it hard to understand what exactly a family life is and needs.'

'The fact that there's no photograph with the four of us in it is quite significant – it's either Sascha with the kids, or me. It's pretty rare to have all of us together.'

'Being married to a colleague from work, works fine for me – taking one's work back home may be a burden to some, but we see it as a great chance to improve the end result. Even the children join in on post work discussions from time to time.'

AHAD ARCHITEKTEN
BRUNSWICK, GERMANY

'The Brunswick region may be a bit provincial compared to cities such as Berlin, but it is economicallyin good shape and there will always be people living in it.'

The office
Location: Brunswick
Owner: Katja and Sascha Ahad
Employees: Sven Wesuls, Jamie Quieser
Founded: 2000
Focus: Single Family Homes

Keywords
Reading matter, sculptural themes, apartment buildings, architecture for the region

'In my opinion one can never experience a space created digitally in 3D in the same way as a space created purely by the hand and mind. The brain understands a lot faster in cooperation with the hand.'

'The first project I produced was the house of my sister... through this work I gained my foundation skills...'

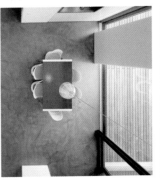

BACHMANN-MÜLLER HOUSE, BRUNSWICK

The project: residence for one family
Location: Schunterterrassen, Brunswick
Builder: private client
Start of planning phase: March 2008
Start of construction: May 2009
Completion: January 2010
Volume: 1,084 m³
Floor area: 340 m² (2 full floors)
Living area: 185 m²
Plot: 598 m²

Construction: reinforced concrete, brickwork
Exterior walls: plaster, wood, oak windows
Floors of coloured cement flooring, parquet oak smoke, stoneware
Photography: Klemens Ortmeyer
Publication: Day of Architecture 2010, touring exhibition 'Low energy', Lower Saxony, Chamber of Architects, 2010, Häuser Portfolio 12/2010, Schöner Wohnen 5/2011

'Often we get calls from construction site management and every so often they ask me if they could please talk to the manager.'

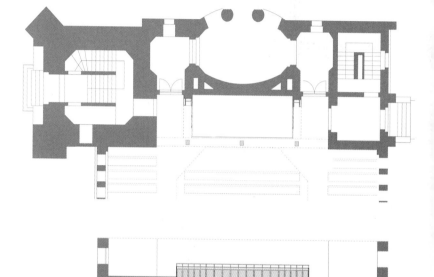

MAIN CHURCH SONNBORN, WUPPERTAL

The project: family church / community café
Location: Sonnborn, Wuppertal
Builder: Protestant Church, Sonnborn, Wuppertal
Start of planning phase: February 2006
Start of construction: June 2006
Completion: September 2006
Construction / Material: coloured screed and plaste, laminated safety glass, sandblasted text, stained oak, wood construction, acoustic ceiling

Photography: Sigurd Steinprinz, Klemens Ortmeyer
Awards: BDA price Wuppertal 2007,
recognition 'Artheon Art Prize' 2008.
Publication: Day of Architecture 2007, 'Building and maintaining', Protestant Church in Rhineland, 2007
BDA Award for Exceptional Buildings 2007
1. Prize: Commendation
children's area and parish cafe at the listed
Church of Sonnborn

KARIN KELLNER
HANOVER, GERMANY

'I am so passionate about my job, it never came to my mind to stay at home to be a full-time mother. No, I think we are so well qualified, it is a part of ourselves. But it still depends on good management, to combine a 4-head family and a job like that. Grandparents and a helpful husband are the keys.'

'Networking is very important, especially when a woman is in maternity leave.'

'Family time is very important to recreate. A solid balance is the best way for creativity.'

'I really enjoy freetime with the 10 grandchildren of my parents, my siblings and the rest of the family on holidays in southern Germany.'

KSW ARCHITEKTEN + STADTPLANER BDA DWB SRL

HANOVER, GERMANY

The office concept is to increase good every-day architecture. Aesthetic requirements combined with a high social responsibility in a contextual design is the focus in every project.

The office
Location: Hanover
Owner: Karin Kellner, Lutz Schleich, Eckhard Wunderling, Matthias Buchmeier
Colleagues: Tim Freund, Sandra Gebauer, Matthias Harms, Anja Iffert, Lena Lindner, Dieter Moje, Johannes Oldenburg, Franziska Roehse, Jörn Schinkel, Jonas Thomann, Sonja Tinney, Marion Voltmer, Frauke Wenninger, Jens Wienhold
Founded: 1991

'Competitions are important to be up-to-date. It is refreshing, to compete and cooperate with new young offices in new challenges!'

Team-working in their office is very important for all of them. The trio prefers working in an atmosphere mixed up with 50/50 % women and men..

The urban framework is the key to successful design..

'In this project we implemented the residents very early in the planning process. In forms of workshops, the architects and residents created think tanks with their knowledge. In this process, I evaluated my today´s most useful skills: **contextual designing**.'

south elevation house 4Q

west elevation house 4Q

SOCIAL HOUSING COMPLEX, SPARGELACKER, HANOVER

The project: social residential buildings
Location: Hanover
Builder: public building authority, GBH (Gesellschaft für Bauen und Wohnen Hannover)
Start of planning phase: 1991
Cooperation: Muth und von der Lage (Architects), Prof. Erich Schneider-Wessling (Köln), GBH
Construction manager: Ansgar Wiegmann
Photos and figures: contributed by the architect

K. Kellner´s work: In cooperation with Muth und von der Lage and Prof. E. Schneider-Wessling 14 5-story buildings, two types of buildings oriented around two town blocks. Over 300 dwelling units were implemented, 48 by KSW. The block structure got opened up. The colour concept played a very important role, to underline the diversity of life in the district.

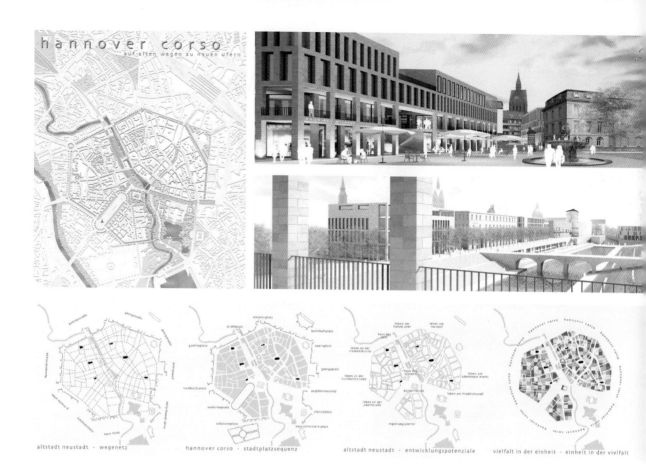

LEINEUFER/HOHES UFER, HANOVER 2020+

The project: urban development, city of Hanover
Builder: public building authority
Location: Leineufer/ Hohes Ufer, Hanover
Cooperation: Nagel, Schonhoff + Partner, Landscape architects, Hanover
Prof. Klaus Scheelhaase, transport planning + urban planning
Prof. Jürgen Collin, transport
Employees: Matthias Buchmeier, Anja Iffert, Jörn Schinkel
Start of planning phase: 2008
Photos and figures: contributed by the architect

Concept: The citycorso will be re-implemented into the city-structure of Hanover, as an already present system, but not yet as noticed figure. The citycorso connects important strategic places, which create the entrée to the following districts and combines the old town centre with the Calenberger Neustadt, with the river Leine and his river banks in the middle of the inner city of Hanover.

BARBARA MARIA
KIRSCH
HANOVER, GERMANY

1988	removal from Munich to Hanover
	little home office – children come first and prove to be more of a challenge to their maybe too conscientious mother than expected
1996	reallocation of office to back yard building around the corner – still children have top priority, so managing a larger office and projects was not possible
2005	appointment of first employee
2010	one employee and an apprentice

'The office's development was largely influenced by the family situation. Project dimensions have remained mainly small scale developments for private clients.
To conclude: bigger projects are virtually impossible with such a family background.'

KIRSCH ARCHITEKTEN
BDA
HANOVER, GERMANY

'The work of architects on small, possibly even unattractive building projects is an important part of building culture.'

The office
Location: Hanover
Owner: Barbara Maria Kirsch and her husband Prof. Albert Schmid-Kirsch
Employees: Gunar Papenberg, Swetlana Kiskin, Annette Ulrich
Founded: 1996 as 'atelier – A – architekten' 2006 renaming in 'kirsch architekten bda'
Focus: old-building renovation

Establish the quality and development opportunities of old buildings and realizing them are one of their specialties. In addition to spatial and aesthetic improvements, they increasingly focus on energy efficient aspects of buildings.

Field of work:
Customer consulting, planning and execution, energy-efficient building and renovation are the centre of gravity of the office.

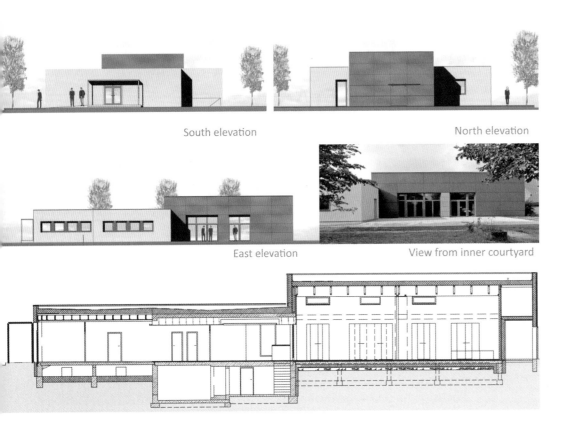

South elevation

North elevation

East elevation

View from inner courtyard

ENERGETIC RENOVATION OF A PARISH HALL – BOTHFELD, HANOVER

The project: energetic renovation of the parish hall 'St. Nicolai' into a passive house
Location: Bothfeld, Hanover -- Germany
Builder: Ev.-luth. St. Nicolai Kirchengemeide
Sponsor: proKlima
Start of planning phase: 2001
Start of construction: September 2006
Completion: 30. September 2007
Photography: Frîa Hagen

The parish hall 'St. Nicolai' was build in 1968. This building needed to be renovated. Therefore the hall on the upper floor had to be removed and reerected in the courtyard at ground level. The rehabilitation of highly insulated walls and roofs is encouraged by proKlima. Triple-glazed windows and ventilation systems with heat recovery lead to heating can be dispensed to own one. The small residual heat is the district heating network of the city-related work.

View of the expansion

Frontage of the entrance area

Group and rest room for children

The wooden cladding

EXPANSION OF A DAYCARE FACILITY FOR CHILDREN – KITA LUENEBURG

The project: expansion of a daycare facility for children
Builder: City of Lueneburg
Location: Lueneburg – Germany
Announcement: Claus Steinnagel, Hanover
Start of planning phase: September 2008
Start of construction: March 2009
Completion: 05. September 2009
Photography: Frîa Hagen

Concept: The existing day-care facility was enhanced by a new annex. Constructed in eco-friendly wood, it connects up to the old building at a slight angle creating a new joint entrance area improving orientation, traffic patterns and utilisation.

Group area and resting space: The wooden cladding creates various light patterns, lights up, but at the same time shields off the interior. Daily work is made more comfortable by carefully planned interior design along with its high quality surfaces.

JOHANNA SIEVERS
HANOVER, GERMANY

'I always wanted to have a big family, that was my dream. Having the family together makes me want to leap for joy. Oh, and by the way: grandchildren are the best thing to have by far!'

SPALINK-SIEVERS
LANDSCHAFTSARCHITEKTEN
HANOVER, GERMANY

'I wasn't born a natural employer, but it's nonetheless going quite well actually – we're celebrating our 20th jubilee this year and are heading down to the south of France for a company outing.'

The office
Location: Hanover
Owner: Johanna Sievers
Employees: 8
Founded: 1991
Focus: Open space planning in renewal areas, private gardens, planning for domestic buildings, planning for residential homes for the elderly, planning for playschools, public spaces and playing fields, school yards, open space planning for administrative buildings

Office philosophy
The office attaches great importance of careful handling with assets. Also public participation is very important. Functionality, clearness in choice of materials and a conclusive, simple design should compose the outside facilities. Good cooperation with clients and architects has to be aspired, for a harmonious unity between buildings and outside facilities. Already in the planning process the aspect of cultivation has to be considered. Cost-conscious and timely working is obligatory.

'Being part of this project as landscape architects right from the beginning was a great honour for us.'

HABITAT – INTERNATIONAL LIVING, HANOVER

The project: 90 living units in council housing: multi-cultural dwelling by integration orientated utilisation concepts
Location: Hanover Kronsberg, Germany
Builder: Gundlach GmbH & Co Wohnungsunternehmen
Start of planning phase: competition 1997, winner: Planungsbüro Schmitz, Aachen
Capacity: 9.3601qm

Open space concept: Strict structuring and design of private, semi private and public spaces. Bowles ground as a community meeting place, private gardens to each ground floor unit.
Photography: Johanna Sievers
Visualisation: M. Bachler, pbs Aachen
Architecture Award of Lower Saxony 2000
Award: Deutscher Spielraumpreis 2000
Publication: 'Habitat – Räume zum Zusammenleben' in: Garten und Landschaft H.8/2000 S. 38

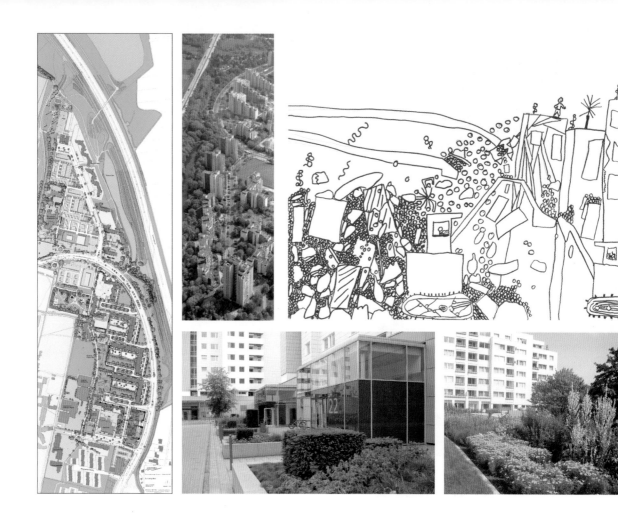

URBAN REDEVELOPMENT WEST: BREMEN OSTERHOLZ – TENEVER, HANOVER

Location: Osterholz-Tenever, Bremen – Germany
Builder: Senator für Umwelt, Bau, Verkehr und Europa, Bremen GEWOBA AG Wohnen und Bauen, Bremen
Start of planning phase: construction competition 2002: 1st prize Architects: Hilmes Lamprecht Architekten BDA, Bremen,
Open space concept competition 2003:
1st prize SPALINK-SIEVERS Landschaftsarchitekten
Completion: 2010

Capacity: 120.000 m²
Publication: 'Grün für Alle – mögliche Antworten der Freiraumplanung auf den demografischen Wandel am Beispiel Bremen-Tenever' in: Garten und Landschaft H.10/2008, S. 18
Award: Bauherrenpreis 2008
Photography: Johanna Sievers
Drawing: Fourth year pupil from Andernachstraße Primary School in Tenever
Aerial view: GEWOBA Bremen

SABINE REBE
HANOVER, GERMANY

'Social architecture has always been my priority.'

'...as I started to study, my daughter went to the first grade of school. It is really quite different when someone doesn`t have children and can fully concentrate on his/her studies. You can work at a different way in an architecture office, having all those stressful tasks and also working on the weekends and still in the evenings... But otherwise I always had the feeling that, if my studies or career didn't go that well, I would still have an important balancing in my life... my family.'

WOHNPLAN
HANOVER, GERMANY

'Times are changing and with them the standards for good living. Wohnplan has specialized in that field of change.'

The office
She usually works alone, but depending of the project and the amount of work gets professional help as a backup (other architects, social psychologists, ergotherapists, etc). Apart from architectural work she researches on security in public spaces.

The concept
Is to increase the autonomy of old or handicapped people who live alone or in a community. Wohnplan is working for housing associations, housing groups and others.

'Wohnberatung (living consultancy)'
Her specialist subject is 'living advice' for housing association's tenants and private customers. She reduces barriers at their domiciles.

The clients
People who have already problems with their living environment and people who take precautions for their old age.

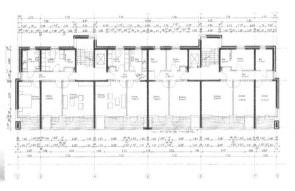

'Flexible spaces
are the future of
architecture.'

ARCHITECTURE, PLANNING, 'WOHNBERATUNG' LIVING CONCEPT GILDE CARREE, HANOVER

The project: a community building without barriers
Builder: the project was built by the Ostland
Wohnungsgenossenschaft eG, Hanover, for Gilde
Carree.
The architects: Hübotter und Stürken,
Architektengemeinschaft BDA
Sabine Rebe's work: Advisory service concerning
community living and living without barriers for
the Gilde Carree project, special: the ground-floors
and details. The layouts of the individual flats were
assessed during a seminar / workshop specially
arranged for the inhabitants to be.

The neighborhood: Streets and pavements are easily accessible for handicapped
people plus there's a Service Center for the elderly on the other side of the street.
The building: The spaces are adapted to all degrees of handicaps. On the ground
floor the common spaces are located: an apartment for the whole community
with a big kitchen, a dining room, a workshop room and two guestrooms.
The apartments: The walls are flexible, so that the inhabitants can choose to
have open spaces or separated rooms. All terraces are connected to the garden
and to one another to increase the social aspect of the project.
There are no level differences between the rooms. The doors and corridors are
wider than 1,20 m (for electric wheelchairs or baby carriage).
Photos and figures: contributed by the architect

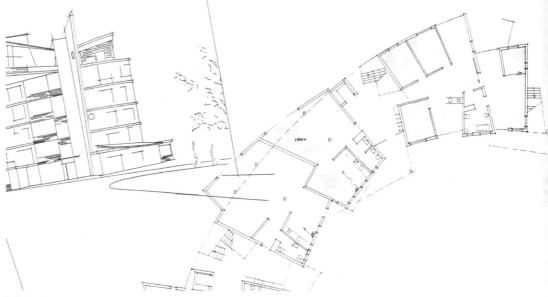

'Each detail in
the plan could
be important to
people's lives.'

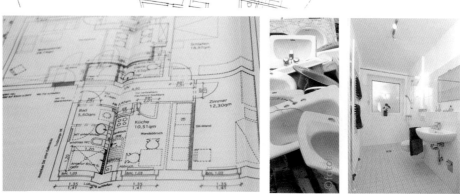

Concepts for housing associations – modernization – barrier reduction – collage of various projects

TOP PICTURES: INNERCITY ESTATE – WOMEN ASSOCIATION, HANOVER

The project: diploma thesis at the Institute of Architecture and Planning Theory; later she was teaching in the same Institute
The authors: Sabine Rebe, Anja Vehrenkamp
Award: Frauenförderpreis, City of Nuremberg in 1996 (Group Practice)
Already as a student Sabine Rebe was always interested in social topics. For the final year project she has picked up 'women – fair accommodation' and she was awarded a prize. That was her first step into her future career. In the year 2001 she wrote a documentation about 'Frauenwohnprojekte in Deutschland' ('Women's housing projects'), edited by the Ministry of the Interior and Sport of Lower Saxony.
Photos and figures: contributed by the architect

BRIGITTE NIESSE
HANOVER, GERMANY

'I have always wanted the two. Fulfilment both at work and at home. Both requires a lot of energy, patience and commitment of two equal partners. Experience and a new awareness of life are two advantages well worth the trouble.'

PLAN ZWEI
HANOVER, GERMANY

'One of the advantages is that we can do what we want
and at the same time want what we do.'

The office
Location: Hanover
Owner: Brigitte Nieße
and her husband Klaus Habermann-Nieße
Employees: Kirsten Klehn, Markus Westhoff, Bettina Schlomka,
Lena Jütting, Simone Müller
Founded: 2005
Focus: Urban planning, urban rehabilitation,
urban district management

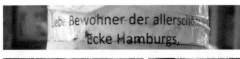

PRELIMINARY STUDY TO A SOCIAL CONSERVATION REGULATION, SCHANZENVIERTEL, HAMBURG

The project: pilot study for a social sustainability establishment
Location: Eimsbüttler Schanzenviertel, Hamburg – Germany
Builder: by order of the economy, construction and environment branch of the Eimsbüttel district council
Completion: October 2010
Photography: office plan zwei

Like many other pre-war inner city housing estates in Hamburg, the Sternschanze is an attractive living area exposed to a tense housing market. The area under investigation already shows many signs of being affected by urban revaluation. This revaluation process has sent rents soaring, as well as the percentage of cooperative apartments whereas the retail industry in the area has decreased dramatically – this and the overall change in residential structure has been heavily criticised. Concerns of an uncontrolled revaluation process squeezing out the local residents have arisen.

URBAN DISTRICT MANAGEMENT DRISPENSTEDT, HILDESHEIM

Location: Drispenstedt, Hildesheim – Germany
Builder: City of Hildesheim
Start of planning phase: 2000
Completion: 2008
Photography: office plan zwei
The project: urban district management – development program 'Soziale Stadt' (social city)

The urban district of Drispenstedt was built in the outskirts of Hildesheim in the 1950s and 1960s.
The communal building company gbg (Non-profit construction company) erected modern, attractive housing estates at that time. Ever increasing demand for council housing had a profound effect on Drispenstedt's urban structure in the following decades. The inclusion in the federal programme 'Urban districts in need of development – the Social City' in 2001 brought along the motto 'Drispenstedt in the ascendency' and the beginning of socio-urban restructuring.

KARIN BUKIES
HANOVER, GERMANY

'Professionals and private fused together, so I also like to work outside.'

'Self-organized trips are part of my free time. The exchange of expertises is extremely important to me.'

'The work in village renewal is satisfying for me because I'm dealing with many different people and experiencing a lot of commitment. At the same time I can make a small contribution to the preservation or the improvement of village environment.'

STADTLANDSCHAFT
HANOVER, GERMANY

'Residents are participating in the planning process. With their local knowledge the recreation process of rural areas has much higher sustainable success. Which is very important, because I do my work to improve THEIR life quality!'

The office
Location: Hanover
Owner: Karin Bukies (Landscape architect)
Dr.-Ing. Harald Meyer (Architect)
Employees: 2 employees, freelancers
Founded: 1984
Focus: urban and landscape planning, regional development and open space planning

The concept
focuses on sustainable and aestetical development. Public participation is very important in the work as well, as rural conservation.

© K.Bukies

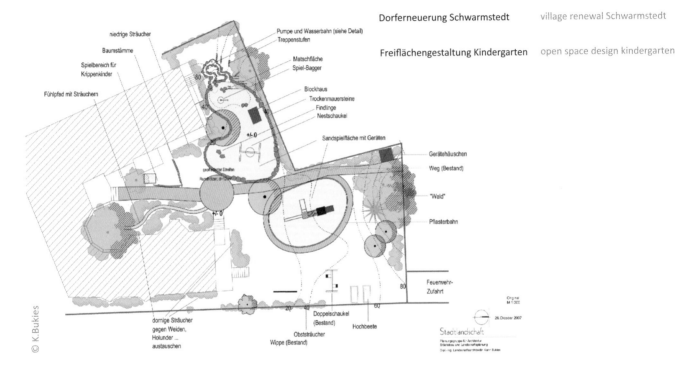

niedrige Sträucher
Baumstämme
Spielbereich für Krippenkinder
Fühlpfad mit Sträuchern

Pumpe und Wasserbahn (siehe Detail)
Treppenstufen
Matschfläche
Spiel-Bagger
Blockhaus
Trockenmauersteine
Findlinge
Nestschaukel
Sandspielfläche mit Geräten

Gerätehäuschen
Weg (Bestand)
"Wald"
Pflasterbahn

Feuerwehr-Zufahrt

dornige Sträucher gegen Weiden, Holunder ... austauschen
Obststräucher
Wippe (Bestand)
Doppelschaukel (Bestand)
Hochbeete

Original M 1:300
26.Oktober 2007
Stadtlandschaft
Planungsgruppe f. Architektur, Städtebau und Landschaftsplanung
Dipl.-Ing. Landschaftsarchitektin Karin Bukies

© K.Bukies

Dorferneuerung Schwarmstedt   village renewal Schwarmstedt

Freiflächengestaltung Kindergarten   open space design kindergarten

PUBLIC PARTICIPATION, SCHWARMSTEDT

The project: It's widely known that public participation and work in planning processes express the ideas and dreams of the local inhabitants best. The overall trend confirms this development. Village renewals mostly being highly user oriented rather than self-fulfilment projects, making participation of the villagers themselves is the most important. The planner needs to thoroughly inform him or herself about the local problems and the area itself to succeed in planning the project. The work groups gather substantial information about the area. Often enough heavy arguments and debates break lose at the work group meeting, but in the end, often lead to various new and alternative ways of dealing with a certain problem. These work groups cultivate the local communication and consensus and improve interior relations. Also, the villagers get to know each other better and even become good friends at times. A whole new feeling of togetherness is created, strongly bonding the local community and enhancing their feeling of identity. Organizing village activities and events like tree planting helps to create a feeling of actively taking part in the process. Changes brought along by this are instantly visible and bring the village together.

Example Hagenhufendorf

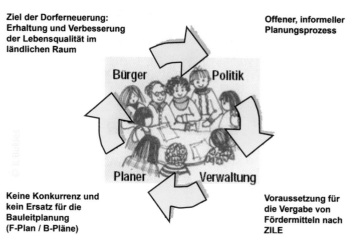

Ziel der Dorferneuerung:
Erhaltung und Verbesserung
der Lebensqualität im
ländlichen Raum

Offener, informeller
Planungsprozess

Bürger Politik

Planer Verwaltung

Keine Konkurrenz und
kein Ersatz für die
Bauleitplanung
(F-Plan / B-Pläne)

Voraussetzung für
die Vergabe von
Fördermitteln nach
ZILE

house stock

mill, Dudensen

streetstructure

RURAL RENEWAL

Karin Bukies makes use of established methods of village renewal projects. A high measure of communication and getting together the young and old are crucial. It's important not to lose sight of the goal: increasing the quality of life for the locals. Economic factors also play an important role in enhancing sustainability.

Karin Bukies encourages the locals to organize and set up work groups. Structuring these groups by topic also helps to achieve a better end result. They develop new ideas and present them to one another in a final meeting. Thereby each idea gets a certain degree of publicity and recognition. People then vote on which of the ideas developed gets to form part of the renewal plan and which ones don't.

Karin Bukies, role during this process is rather of an advisory nature, because the villagers usually know their local area and it's needs best. She does however raise awareness especially in questions of design.

NILOUFAR M. ALIHA
TEHRAN, IRAN

'Thanks to the support of my family and husband, two months after my child was born I could go to work again. Yet as a mother many times I have to choose between my family and work. My family is always my first priority for sure.'

Part Ham-Gorouh Andish Architects

'I look to the subjects of my pictures closely.
Through photography I like to study the construction and texture of materials. But I don't care much about the frames.'

'In general, old cultural behaviours combined with religious views both act as obstacles for women to achieve equality with men in society ...'

One woman, two worlds

'It's quite normal that conflicts occur in big projects with different groups working together (architects, civil engineers, mechanical engineers, etc ....) and I am, luckily, very capable of being able to moderate between parties to solve the problem.'

Sports Stadium Ardabil, Iran
Location: City of Ardabil – north west of Iran
Capacity: 6000 seats (+1500 standing)
football, handball, basketball, volleyball, gymnastics and wrestling (flexible-use)
The building has three main sections:
I. viewers II. play ground III. installation
Photos and figures: contributed by the architect

'Understanding the geometry and function of the space is very important to me.'

JANNINA CABAL
GUAYAQUIL, ECUADOR

'... to be as groundbreaking as possibly in every single project we work on. We just don't want to settle with a simply okay looking project.

We study the area, taking into consideration the sun's influence, the weather and obviously the client's needs. My line of architecture as you see is vanguard, due to the materials I use. However, the organic materials such as stone or wood, give the projects a traditional reference. I have been inspired by modern architecture and also cubism – but local traditions, customs and weather have always strongly influenced my work.'

Jannina Cabal Arquitectos
Jannina has been married since she was 23 and she has 3 children. Her husband helps her and works in an architecture related area. Her mother helps checking her children's homework while she is out of town.

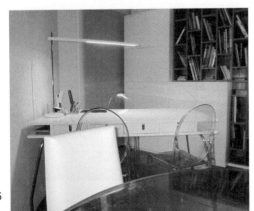

'...the other day while making drafts for a park project here in Guayaquil, I sat next to my son and he started giving me ideas of how great it would be to experience passing through the water to enter the place and to feel like you are on the beach. Things like that make you think differently, make you see things through different eyes. My children have inspired me I think! They always keep giving me fresh ideas!'

'...sustainable design means relating people with their natural environment, complying with the principles of economic, social and ecological sustainability in the majority of projects if possible.' J. Cabal

CASA MANOSALVAS, GUAYAQUIL

Manosalvas house sits majestically and vibrantly between purely architectonic elements and the public square.

The building's structure and volumes are easy to make out on it's facade. On the inside however, it produces a large variety of contrasts, some by shape, some by surface and some by both.

Stone elements surround and divide the entrance area from the staircase and ribbon glazed windows. The visual impact enhances the innovative way that individual spaces are connected together, creating a unique architectonic experience.

Photos and figures: contributed by the architect

EVA M. ÁLVAREZ ISIDRO
VALENCIA, SPAIN

gómez+álvarez arquitects
Our work has been produced without giving up our basic ideals. From the very beginning, and even against the main strand, we thought our academic work should be centred on the students' learning; our professional one should be supported by dignity; our ethic compromise should rely in positive action. We also wanted to take care of our family unit. And we manage to simultaneously tackle all these work spheres during these years. Though it has not been planned, this personal position has shown us clear ways to drive our activity. And now, when looking back, we guess this is our strongest value: We are involved in a different way of looking at architecture, urban design and academics. Nowadays, this interaction is called gender approach to urbanism and architecture, topic we are totally interested in.

'As an architect I always thought about gender issues, without realizing that this thoughts belong to gender topics.'

MASSANASSA TOWNHALL, SPAIN
Project: Massanassa townhall
Location: Massanassa, Spain
Promotion: Massanassa municipality
Builder: Francisco Vidal SL
Start of planning phase: 1995
Completion: 2003
Photography: Carlos Gómez

The old school of 'Ausias March' and its grounds have been the focus of this rehabilitation project and were turned into Massanassa's new town hall and public square. This development process included designing street furniture and the entire interior furniture from scratch.
Ultimately finished in November 2003, the project had gone through five successive construction phases, each of them funded by one global budget pool.
The building was constructed in the 1930s, has a high emotional factor and is an icon to the people of the village.

SHEILA SRI PRAKASH
CHENNAI, INDIA

Architecture is a family business. Her husband, son, daughter, son in law and daughter in law work in this field. Her daughter Pavitra studied architecture and works in the office as a planner. Her husband coordinates the integration of engineering to architecture for all projects. He also is in charge of the administration, though he is a chemical engineer but he has been exposed to this field for a long time. Her son and son in law invest money on projects.

Shilpa Architects + Planners + Designers Pvt. Ltd
Founded Shilpa Architects in Chennai, India
Sheila Sri Prakash is among the first women in India to start and operate their own office.

'As a professional dancer, think that I can feel the space better than others. I can understand the flow of space and see behind of it. During the performances and the interaction with audiences, I could understand the connection between space and audiences and develop it to the architecture and users.'

'Creating spaces is a big responsibility. As nature was given to us by the Almigthy, if we change it , it should happen in a positive way. I believe that a well created space can, especially from a psychological point of view, motivate people to become better people.'

MAHINDRA WORLD CITY, MITL, CHENNAI, INDIA

Mahindra World City is one of the first Special Economic Zone´s (SEZ´s) in Chennai with over 600 acres. Within World City a fully fledged research facility has been planned, completed with the required Residential Program to support Mahindra Research Valley's staff. This 27 acre master plan has been designed in phases to incorporate the research staff in traditional dwelling units as well as hostel type units on site.

Admin Block:
The administration block for Mahadushi International Trade Ltd (MITL) finished in 2008 is the first building that springs into view when entering Mahindra World City. The developer was looking for a 'gatehouse' that was both iconic in structure and design and a functional office.

Photos and figures: contributed by the architect

Railway Station:
PARANUR RAILWAY STATION is the busy transit train station within Mahindra World City. This project was completed in partnership with the Indian Railways and was handed over in December 2007.

MARIA VIÑÉ and
MARTINA VOSER

ZURICH, SWITZERLAND

'Over time one figures out that sacrifices inevitably have to be made when it comes to combining work and family life. Everyone needs to set their own priorities and decide what's most important in their lives and what they might be able to do without from time to time.'

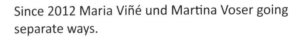

Since 2012 Maria Viñé und Martina Voser going separate ways.

The office «vi.vo.architektur.landschaft gmbh» is rebranded into «mavo gmbh» with Martina Voser.

Maria Viñé founded her new office «Neuland ArchitekturLandschaft GmbH» in Zürich.

'Undoubtedly, the building industry is still a male dominated field of expertise – women are still very underrepresented. Clinically though, chances of succeeding are equal, but one does have to consider that women get confronted with the same old clichés and are struggling to live up to expectation levels considerably higher than the ones of their male co-workers.'
M. Viñé

'The earlier architects and landscape architects start working together, the better because inside and outside spaces begin to intersect more naturally and fluently.'

RESIDENTIAL SETTLEMENT TRIEMLI, ZURICH
competition 1st prize
Builder: construction cooperative Sonnengarten
Architects: Ballmoos Krucker Architekten
Cooperation: Nadia Buhlmann, Susanne Donaubauer
Planning: 2006–2009
Photos and figures: contributed by the architects

The urbanistic outline generates an interior space of both residence and passage as well as an outer crust which reacts dimensionally to its respective urban counterpart. Üetlibergwald forest and the residential gardens are vegetationaly connected.

LIDEWIJ TUMMERS
ROTTERDAM, THE NETHERLANDS

She prioritizes the flexibility to travel over the stability of family life.

Tussen Ruimte operates as an interdisciplinary network, developing inclusive and sustainable approaches to architecture and urbanism. Collaborating in a wide range of projects, from urban renewal, experiments with re-use of building material after demolition and integration of renewable energies in architecture to design workshops and art installations or documentaries.

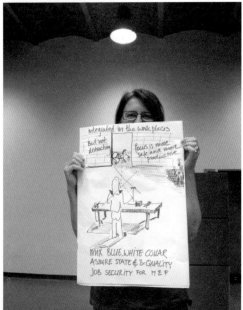

Slow Architecture:

'Processes of design and creation require careful attention, experimentation
and enough time to build insight, confidence and collaboration.
Every project needs an in-between space where exploration and growth
can happen, as fundamental elements of sustainability.'

L. Tummers

Participative design: POORTGEBOUW

Core Values

Since its founding in 1999, Tussen Ruimte has build a
network with reliable firms and experts around Europe
and beyond dedicated to create 'slow architecture'
and reducing the ecological footprint of the built
environment. Think global, act local: the more we
reduce our footprint, the further we walk. We are
committed to practice-as-we-preach.

The project

'Poortgebouw' is the name of a monumental building
as well as of the association of its inhabitants.
Since 1983 they form a collective of young artists,
professionals and students living and working in the
building they rent as a collective. In 2001 the building
was sold to a private developer who aims to re-develop
it for office space. Besides taking the eviction-order to
court the Poortgebouw Collective have also developed
a renovation plan of their own. Tussen Ruimte
organised workshops to articulate future spatial needs
and provided technical solutions. Jointly, a feasible
plan was produced that attracted new partners for the
collective.

Photos and figures: contributed by the architect
http://www.tussen-ruimte.nl/

monumental fassade

Designworkshop

the attic, model

detailed plans

Tussen Ruimte

VALENCIA VALENCIA

on stage! exhibition>>valencia stop
another way of looking at architecture
landscape architecture and planning
>>gender mainstreaming

international workshop>>
2 cr free election
march-may 2012
information>> february,29th at 11 am
place>> 524 classroom
more on facebook>>

© Eva Álvarez and Carlos Gómez

© Eva Álvarez and Carlos Gómez

ON STAGE! VALENCIA, STOP 2012

by Eva Álvarez and Carlos Gómez

On Stage! exhibition was designed to travel and to be increased with new material, as long as wished. So, this way, it could compile the actual state of the question OUT THERE, RIGHT NOW, since we noticed how difficult showing women architects' work is by current media; even more, how difficult showing a new perspective on women's work is... And no need to say how difficult showing the present state of the professional situation for women (and men) is... Consequently, this new material ought to proceed from a deep research in the place the exhibition was going to visit.

So, after Hanover exposition finished, the panels shown were transported to Valencia and we completed them with new and original material developed by architects and master students at the School of Architecture at Universitat Politècnica de València (UPV). Our goals were to research, show and assess women architect's work from a gender perspective. Following this target, we conducted a students' work seminar during March, April and May 2012, in order to decide the way we wanted to show women's work, and we invited the architects selected to participate, with a view to designing and producing the new material to be exhibited in Valencia. It should be mentioned that the architects selected who had an exceptional curriculum, were prepared to work for free with us because we knew them from different academic or professional contexts... and, of course, because they were also friends of ours.

To pursue this research purpose, we proposed a non hierarchic way to work: each opinion or idea, by students or architects, should be argued, debated and agreed. During this collective work, soon the questions of time and social fabric arose.

With regard to TIME, it became visible to us that women (and men) have to share time and decide the cost in time each activity has and deserves; so, organizing time turns into one of the most valuable tasks for each person. Professional and personal lives are entangled: working time is also personal time; activities done under personal time are able to provide new scopes or shed new light on professional decisions. So we proposed to show professional and personal time INTERTWINED.

Regarding SOCIAL FABRIC, we had to debate more: one of us wanted to show individual profiles; others wanted to show a collective photo since, it was argued, professional and personal possibilities and capabilities depend on collective development: We can study because someone before us built the educational system and all its infrastructure; we can move because we use a collective infrastructure for mobility formed by from highways to small streets. We can live in society because society was organized by someone else... Every personal achievement is backed by a collective development.

After different sessions debating on these topics, we decided to show a unique panorama, a unique image where all selected architects and times were presented together. And also, at the same time, we wanted to use a common questionnaire or interview of agreed questions, in order to make pop up personal experiences or personal sentiments around (or together) professional development (the responses date from May 2012).

Thinking in the way to show these ideas, we arrived at the notion of metro lines: different trains and persons moving in a collective space, but perfectly identified. Travel paths are able to coincide (as for example in Valencia on May 18th, 2012) or diverge. It can be programmed (in the case of trains) or it can be fortuitous (in the case of personal travels).

So, we all worked intensely. Architects provided us with personal and professional data and images, and they carefully answered our questionnaire which we reproduce here. Students and teachers decided the formal layout – as requested by the authors of this text – and we all produced ALL the material. We received economic support from the School of Architecture, the Architectural Projects Department and the PV.

The vernissage was made to coincide with a two-day international seminar which was given the same title. We invited Barbara Zibell, Doris Damyanovic, Inés Novella and Bárbara Pons to attend, who all debated on different aspects of women architects' work. The vernissage session, on May 18th, 2012, in one of the deepest moments of the economic recession in Spain, was enlivened by a live concert presented by students attending the seminar, together with friends of them. They all play in important orchestras... We were proud of this moment of happiness and commitment.

On Stage! Valencia Stop
Coordinators: Eva Álvarez and Carlos Gómez
Architects: Inés Moisset, Lizete Rubano, Agata Dzianach, Marilda Azulay, Inés Novella, Cristina Alonso, Lola Domènech
Students: Bianny Poueriet, Natalia Ulloa, Elizabeth Méndez, Ana Patricia Cruz, Ariel Perea, Ainara Cuenca, Simona Lasauskaite, Maryia Kukharava, Iradani Katalia
English translation: Simona Lasauskaite, Eva Álvarez
Concert organization: Ainara Cuenca
Seminar lecturers: Barbara Zibell, Doris Damyanovic, Inés Novella, Bárbara Pons
Economic support: UPV, School of Architecture, Architectural Projects department

A. INÉS MOISSET, CÓRDOBA, ARGENTINA

Inés Moisset

a) About the current personal and/or family situation: The architect will tell us what she considers relevant about the current situation.
There's not much to be said, just my parents are architects (already retired) and my current associate was my husband.

b) About the point of view of the architecture before the studies: memories of the architectural experiences before the studies started, the point of view at that time (Thinking Architecture, Zumthor).
I was always seeing what my parents were doing at the office and at the university. Since I was a little girl I used to go with them to lectures at the faculty. We travelled a lot with my parents visiting A LOT of pieces of architecture. My mother teaches History of Architecture. At the age of eight I knew that I wanted to go on with architecture and become part of the university.

c) About the formation as an architect: How did the years of the studies go, what topics/assignments/circumstances had the most influence on your motivation for studies, what do you think now about that period of life, what would you change and what not, what was the political, economic and cultural background at that moment?
It was a very stimulating period, after the end of the dictatorship, but economically difficult. In 1989 Argentina went through a big hyperinflation crisis that led to an institutional one. Since it was impossible to purchase anything, because the currency was devalued in a matter of hours, we used to gather materials from the streets with classmates to make our models. I also remember when we visited Currutchet House in La Plata, it was a revealing moment. I studied at the National University of Córdoba, which had a very good level by that time, excellent professors. Among them I can mention Horacio

Gnemmi, with whom I started to be an assistant student, and mainly César Naselli, with whom I collaborated later at his Arquitectura IV chair and in his research projects. Naselli developed some research about the design process and creativity, and his workshops were very stimulating. All that enhanced the establishment of a group of similar people with great enthusiasm. Naselli's teams from National University and Catholic University started to gather every Saturday to develop creative experiences. That is where Instituto de Diseño was born, in 1990, a research seminar on design principles (together with Viviana Colautti, Esteban Bondone and Ian Dutari).

d) About the beginning of the professional activities: What did you choose to do in that moment, what influence did this choice have on your current work, what problems/advantages did it generate, what was the political, economic and cultural background at that moment?
Just after I was graduated, I was lucky enough to be called by Marina Waisman to collaborate with her in the chair of *Problemática de la Modernidad en América Latina*. Marina is the region's most important architecture critic, and she was especially concerned at the education of the young people and thus she formed the Centre for the Education of Researchers in Architectural History, Theory and Critics, in which I was involved for several years being in charge of editing its magazine.

On the other hand, I started to work for Togo Díaz office, a local architect with a particular, very sensitive and careful work, but also for a construction company which completely changed a part of the city: Nueva Córdoba. Togo built over 200 buildings in Córdoba, during the time I worked in his office. I took part in 7 projects for high-rise residential buildings, apart from other works like a shopping centre, some single-family houses, a hotel, etc.

In parallel, I kept on collaborating with César Naselli at Instituto del Diseño, where I started to do research into

fractals. César encouraged me to apply for a grant so I could develop this work more formally, and I finally got it from the Consejo de Investigaciones de la Provincia de Córdoba, between 1994 and 1998.

Thus, I had the chance to share work with three references of Latin American architecture. Motivated by César and Marina, in 1997 I moved to Italy to do a doctorate at the Istituto Universitario di Architettura di Venezia, which I finished in 2000. Here, theoretical training completed the practicing I brought from Argentina. I met many people of great worth among my classmates, and we started our first online collaborations. Students from Italy, Germany, Austria, Korea and other nationalities gather in doctorate courses. From there we formed, together with Omar Paris, Red Hipótesis de Paisaje which organized seminars for 10 years without a break.

In December 2001, in the frame of another crisis in our country ('corralito') we decided together with Omar to edit the first book of Editorial i+p (investigación + proyecto), taking advantage of our editorial experience in the MW magazine (from Marina Waisman Centre). It was a thoughtless thing because any economic analyst would have said that it had to be stopped, but it went well since the currency was devaluated and it was difficult to import books from abroad, they were so expensive that we had no competitors at the beginning. There was barely any publishing production in Argentina about architecture, so crisis turned to opportunity. Obviously it was impossible to build by that time, and most of our university mates emigrated.

In 2004, we decided to publish 30–60 Cuaderno Latino-americano de Arquitectura, a periodical publication with a meticulous selection of contents where we suggest less evident glances over contemporary architecture works from Latin America. The name 30–60 refers to a geographical position; these numbers are Northern and Southern parallels between which Latin America is located (from Mexico to Patagonia). In 8 years of activity we have promoted the construction of collective knowledge. Over 400 collaborators have participated, providing a wide and varied glimpse. Works are selected by an international committee giving preference to emerging trends. Critics are especially invited to review works from a constructive approach. There are more than 200 works and more than 200 texts within the 32 issues that have been published constituting an enhancement for new ideas. This enterprise needs business logic to stay alive, something about we weren't educated and we had to obtain through training and consulting.

e) About the current situation of your professional activities: What opinion do you have about it, have you imagined your future doing exactly what you are doing now, how did you benefit from your cultural and personal legacy, how does the political, economic and cultural background affect you at the moment?
Apart from my research and writing in 30–60, I currently work at Carrera de Investigador Científico de CONICET, where I have been working full-time since 2002. Carrera de Investigador Científico y Tecnológico is a national body that gathers all those who do creative research and development from different levels of conception, design, approach and practice of all scientific disciplines. There, I work in fields related to public space and to alternative research methodologies bound to our discipline. I am responsible for leading projects and training human resources (PhD candidates). I also teach in some postgraduate courses, especially from Latin America. Besides, I coordinate Innovative Design Processes Master in Universidad Católica de Córdoba, where all above researches take place and where designers from different disciplines meet.

I find my job very stimulating, although it isn't the professional profile shown in the schools of architecture. The possibilities of our disciplines are much wider than the university programs. The space and funding given by our nation to generate science and technology is something to emphasize, especially when there is a lack of available resources. The stability achieved during the last years made possible to bear an editorial project that was born in a crisis. Furthermore, there are so many things to be resolved and so much room to make proposal (in all fields). That is an open door to creativity.

f) About other non-paid complementary activities: How do they relate to your current work, what advantages and disadvantages do they generate, in what way do they influence your point of view?
I cooperate with some civic participation groups and heritage protection groups, which demands to be on permanent alert and to provide information to media. The advantage is to have the chance to have a bearing on politics, avoiding that the knowledge stays within the universities and academic circles. This allows interacting with media, politicians, social organizations, etc. and it provides a broader vision than the one given by the discipline.

g) About the compatibility between different kinds of activities: How do you achieve it, does it generate any problem or the advantage for you?
So far there are no incompatibilities. Everything I do is different sides of the same thing.

h) About the visibility and recognition of your work and other non-paid activities: Do you feel well compensated for your efforts and professional capacity, do you consider you have equal opportunities, or do you have to choose?
I cannot complain about myself. I am a privileged. I am where I want to be, in the fight.

i) About the social point of view of the work made by women: Do you consider the behavior as fair, do you share your responsibilities with your familiars and/or partners, do you find the language used around you to be discriminatory?

I never felt offended by any of my workmates or relatives; neither in the institutions I am working. But this is within the academic and scientific spheres where I move and with the personal. On the contrary, I was always encouraged. I cannot extend this to the whole social perception of the labour made by women or the whole architecture profession. But I do take questions about why I chose not to be a mother, since it's what is expected from a woman. Obviously responsibilities like reproduction, maternity and care are made invisibly and with no room for discussion. Besides, construction is a sphere where masculine prevails. Female students have little references in that sense.

j) About the incorporation of the gender perspective to the everyday life: Do you consider that it is necessary to intensify collective incorporation of the gender perspective, do you think that this particular action would bring any improvement (or not), please describe in what way it would affect you?

I totally agree with the introduction of the gender mainstream to everyday life. That would mean more equitable relationship between the sexes. Even if I consider myself an exceptional case, I don't work alone, but I network with many other people where disparity is present and not alien to me. Obviously, the problem should be solved as society and not as something isolated.

k) About the existence of 'different way of seeing the architecture': Do you consider that there are different points of view, what is your opinion about it, do you think it is positive to insist at this particular point?

Absolutely, and it is very valuable if we have an approach from which we assume that diversity is the richness of our society. It is also necessary to say that gender perspective is not only a women issue but it has to be debated by men who will gain other roles. Besides, it is impossible to separate this debate from a criticism of capitalism (and the issue of labour) and the sustainability of our planet. Even if they seem topics of great magnitude they are completely linked to everyday private decisions.

l) About the possible prognosis of the near future: How do you see the professional situation in short/long terms, how do you see the social situation of women in short/long terms, do you see any alternatives in professional work of the architects?

I think there are great opportunities for women architects if we consider a redefinition of the profession. This redefinition means rethinking the way we build, the technology, the times, the stakeholders of the system; and those areas where women are more present (research, theory and critics) should be introduced into university programs. This is a micro scale where we can act and have effect.

© Inés Moisset

Lizete Rubano

B. LIZETE RUBANO, SÃO PAULO, BRASIL
A few comments about the inquiry …

Maybe, some issues about my personal life would be interesting in order to identify the options and traces which led me to where I am now.

One of the most important issues is the story of my own family: their humble origin as Italian immigrants, leaving their country in a postwar period and their change from farmers to inhabitants in central São Paulo. From Vale Dell' Angelo to Bixiga… The third generation achieved, by the commitment of the first ones, the possibility of attending university.

The path followed by public schools is also an important part of this story, since after the military dictatorship – that devastated the country for twenty years – they never regained the quality of education. But when I was in the school and in high school, we had philosophy, music, excellent teachers…

From 1964 to 1976, the MEC-USAID agreements (between Education – Cultural Ministry and United States Agency for International Development) transformed the structure of the educational system in Brazil, reducing the timetable of critic disciplines (some of them were even eliminated) and changing the basic values of our education, which went on to return to the market.

But it was in the public school before the reformation, where we had an enviable educative structure (I hardly even realized I was living the last years of that experience), when I decided to study architecture: the most free profession, the one which would allow me having more freedom than any other… that's what I thought at that time and that's the reason why I chose it.

That impression (or, that desire) soon was showing not to be exactly untrue, but – at least – distant from everyday, first in the context of formation, as it came from a more traditional school and, in many aspects, less critical and more professional.

Passing the entrance examination of Architecture and Urbanism Faculty at the Presbyterian Mackenzie Institute (in 1977) brought me a different experience, a different one to what my education process had been until that point: teachers who preferred hierarchy, students with different (higher) income, university student group's reactions, claiming for democratic freedom (we then lived in a state of exception). One only had to cross Maria Antonia Street to fall in the confrontation between Social Sciences progressive students at USP and the conservative students of the CCC ('Chase of Communists Command'), present in several faculties at University. Architecture also showed resistance to that conservative movement.

While there was a total strangeness with that people universe, things and issues, I also started to change my affections, tastes, causes with the final purpose of fighting for the rights of citizenship and making it the goal of my profession.

My final project was developed about the Serra do Bananal squatters, in Peruíbe, south coast of São Paulo. Due to the news in journals, I identified a dispersed community in the mountain that planted bananas and sold at a price well above that of the purchase by brokers who took them to Santos market (Santos is another coastal town, São Paulo south).

Working with the farmer's reality and their housing conditions (in this case we used the 'pau-a-pique' technique) was highly important for what came after: the election of a political party (to militate) and the aim of my professional activity – frail lands and collective housing. Very significant for the choice of a party (the Workers' Party) was reading the text: 'The question of the Party' in 1981.

As an additional education, I attended some university courses in philosophy, literature and human sciences at USP, as an occasional student. I chose subjects in sociology and anthropology. José de Souza Martins and Renato Silva Queiroz were some of the teachers with whom I became closer in that time.

In this occasion, my personal interest for rural life led me to read and learn about some classics which have been essential in my personal formation. Due to that interest I developed my master degree, which started in 1986 and it was completed in 1992 in the USP, Faculty of Architecture and Urbanism. With the title: *'The working and living conditions for agricultural farmers and workers: Study case in Marilia municipality.'* Changing from rural to urban spheres was a no way back leap. By different reasons, the city, the concentrations, the periphery occupation became my favorite (and necessary) topic.

Some of my professional experiences were very strong: working in the committee of operations, at that time at the COHAB-SP (Companhia Municipal de Habitação); during the period 1989–1992 with the management of Luiza Erudina. For the first time, the Workers' Party came to power and with it also the possibility to do what we had studied and argued, what encouraged all of us.

Another experience, along with GAMHA (Advisory Group for Habitat Movements) from 1995 to 1997, deserves being mentioned as well. First of all, regarding urban plot subdivision and housing typology works along with Prefectural of San José (Interior of São Paulo) and later, because of refurbishment projects and works monitoring in various buildings (homes and locals businesses).

My academic career, now as a professor of Architectural Design at the Faculty of the year that I was hired by the Mackenzie Presbyterian University, where I am working till this day.

Universidade Presbiteriana Mackenzie

A pesquisa CRÍTICA RADICAL À METRÓPOLE: ENSAIOS E PROJETAÇÃO estabeleceu como objetivo investigar **possibilidades de projeto** – urbano e arquitetônico – que representassem alternativas – **intelectuais e de ação** – à **condição da cidade do negócio**, à cidade que se faz, inclusive com suas arquiteturas, a partir de lógicas que restringem o acesso à dimensão pública.

Dadas as **alterações estruturais** no **mundo contemporâneo** (forma de produzir a vida material, "revolução" da informação, novas condições colocadas ao público/privado e às associações tempo/espaço, dentre outras), perguntávamo-nos **quais seriam as condições possíveis ao projeto (pensamento e prática)** quais as possíveis reflexões - e propostas – que têm contabilizado essas temáticas, como poderiam ser identificadas e quais proposições têm representado exercícios no sentido de se reencontrar (ou criar) oportunidades efetivas (com significado e valor) de projeto.

Quais seriam, por exemplo, as possibilidades de se elaborar uma arquitetura suporte com um adensamento programático baseado em oposições, conflitos, tensões e não em hierarquias opressivas ou de rechaço ao imprevisível e informal. Ou ainda, quais as possibilidades de intervenções suportes que estimulassem a interrogação do usuário e fossem capazes de "responder" às solicitações, estruturas de hospitalidade incondicional, não seletivas ou inibidoras?

O que fizemos, a partir de levantamento em periódicos, (uma das referências públicas da discussão de projetos para a cidade), foi selecionar artigos e escolher projetos que representassem possibilidades diferenciadas à cidade, a partir de duas formulações - e escalas - abrangentes : há intervenções urbanas que promovem e potencializam ações, através de conflitos e tensões programáticas, movimentos contínuos de desterritorializações e reterritorializações, incentivando o nomadismo, as conexões momentâneas extrínsecas, ou seja, fora da natureza do lugar, entre margens, nas bordas. **As micro-políticas do lugar**. Essa era uma possibilidade que apontávamos à própria condução da pesquisa.

A uma outra questão, mais ligada à **macro-política territorial**, estariam associadas às ações estruturadoras de uma diversa "ordem" de valores e possibilidades à vida na cidade.Que se apresentassem como condições espaciais importantes, qualificadoras de urbanidades democráticas.

Estas duas escalas pareciam ser complementares .

Adotamos, para o recorte temporal, o ano de 1995, momento em que se deu a primeira bienal exclusiva de arquitetura, como um momento que, por este fato, poderia ser uma expressão de que a disciplina ganhava um importante espaço de discussão.

Ensaística e indagativa, a pesquisa elegeu algumas situações na cidade que se apresentam, tanto como micro-políticas locais como macro-políticas territoriais, como possibilidades de uma outra história dentro da própria história.

REALIZAÇÃO 2008
PROFESSORES PESQUISADORES DA FAU MACKENZIE
Dra. Lizete Maria Rubano (Coordenação da Pesquisa)
Dr. Igor Guatelli (Pesquisador PPI)
Doutorando Lucas Fehr (Pesquisador PPI)
Dra. Maria Isabel Villac (Pesquisador PPI)
Dr. Mario Figueroa (Pesquisador PPI)
Doutorando Marcelo Barbosa (Pesquisador Voluntário)

ALUNOS BOLSISTAS
Carolina Lunetta; Fabio Ucella; Aline Simões Oltertz Silva; Mayara Rocha Christ; Thais Velasco; Felipe de Freitas Moreira;Bruno Cannavale Atra

PESQUISADORES VOLUNTÁRIOS
André Cossi Navarro; Andrea Key Abe; Vinícius Stump; Yara Pereira;Fernanda Lima Sakr; Maraisa Ramos; Guilherme Ortenblad; Tatiana Fuentes; Simone Gatti;

Este trabalho foi financiado pelo **Mack Pesquisa**

© Lizete Rubano

My PhD was completed in 2001, also in FAUUSP on an issue that later will take a lot of my time: *'Project Culture: Study of ideas and proposals for collective housing'.*

There were selected some collective habitat projects, realized in the twentieth century between Brazil (São Paulo) and the Netherlands (Amsterdam), parting from the idea of building a "Culture Project" that would guide the contemporary production considering the relationship between habitability and cities. We prepared project sheets, organized in two teams. However, after going through many semesters of graduation where the budget cuts have influenced mainly building and its technological components, I was invited to join the 7th and 8th semesters, in which we worked on the topic *"The urban dimension of each and any project action"*. Thus, we introduced a role of urban design and the commitment in academic formation, even when considering each intervention as something punctual, creating the cities.

Since 2005, Mackenzie University offered professors the opportunity to make a real academic career path: a research possibility. Since then, I have been working on the dimension of the project – as theoretical-critical reflection and as action – parting from the perspective of an alleged distance, identified between discipline and Brazilian urban territory reality: long time ago, we abandoned the city. The beautiful building placed in the middle of nowhere on four pillars – it was our recognized product to export.

Our cities, generic for, maybe, different reasons to the ones by Koolhaas in 2004, represent the worst legacies for our urban experience, and have no way back. A periphery conformed by an absence of urbanism and self-construction which spreads and matches as our way of 'making city', by infilling in historical fabric (still a recent history) or by composing expansion areas, beyond the condo ghettos and 'global' territories.

Under this perspective, two researches were conducted: in 2007–2008, *'Radical critic of metropolis: essays and projects'* and in 2010–2011, *'An action in the city: urbanism in critical areas. Proposals and methods by architect Hector Vigliecca and team'.* Both studies were supported by Mackesquisa. And in both investigations, the goal was to observe the capacity to generate, reassign and empower urban places.

CROQUIS CORTE

© Lizete Rubano

© Lizete Rubano

My home is at your disposal if you wish to visit São Paulo...

© Agata Dzianach

Agata Dzianach

© Agata Dzianach

C. AGATA DZIANACH, POLAND

a) About the current personal and/or family situation: The architect will tell us what she considers relevant about the current situation.

I got married in April of my third year of studies of the Interior Design. My husband is an electrical engineer. Our daughter Jula was born during the vacations after the third year of my second studies. During these vacations, I decided to start working as a freelancer in the field of interior and furniture. So in the last two years of my studies, I was trying to unify being a student, making freelance projects and being a mother. Now my girl is four years old. While still being in Poland, I had no problem with my work: I made projects for private clients, always because of previous recommendations. Now, after moving to Galicia, I continue working more as an architect/artist (thanks to a wide professional field) than interior designer. Together with my husband, we are initiating some more multifunctional projects (related with urbanism), taking advantage of the possible and interesting combination of our professions.

b) About the point of view of the architecture before the studies: memories of the architectural experiences before the studies started, the point of view at that time (Thinking Architecture, Zumthor).

I haven't imagined myself studying something else. I was quite sure to study what I had chosen in the first place.

c) About the formation as an architect: How did the years of the studies go, what topics/assignments/circumstances had the most influence on your motivation for studies, what do you think now about that period of life, what would you change and what not, what was the political, economic and cultural background at that moment?

I started my adventure with the Academy in the course of 2003/2004. It was not Architecture, but Education of Arts. After the first year there, I started the Interior Design classes in the same School. For two years I was studying two courses at the same time – one was a Degree in Arts, which I studied for 3 years and finished in 2007; and another – Degree in Interior Design, finished in 2010 after 5 years of studying (at that time we didn't have the Bologna system in my Academy, it's quite new in Poland – the students who initiated their studies two years after I did, already started with this system). The studies for me where 'super' difficult and till this moment I think my bravest choice was to take various specialties, which I was lucky to be able to do. Despite this fact, I understood quite early that the most important is the practice. That's why, after my second year in School, I decided to go to a small studio of an architect in order to see how it is all done in practice. It is what the formation is lacking – the contact with reality. Thanks to my decision to start working so early, I was able to work during my last three years of studies. It gave me the security in being responsible for the construction works.

While studying I was thinking that you have to always understand that everything depends on you, no matter if there is unemployment in your profession or not, and that nobody ever promised you that you will have a job. I think it is true right now as well. Another thing I valued a lot in my studies is the quantity of students in one group (just 15) and a close contact with the professors (it was not anonymous) – it allows you to study without any stress. But if it's not you who takes care of your professional development, no one else will. The studies are for showing you the possibilities you may have but they don't give you assurance of whether you will have a job or not.

d) About the beginning of the professional activities: What did you choose to do in that moment, what influence did this choice have to your current work, what problems/advantages did it generate, what was the political, economic and cultural background at that moment?

I started to work in practice as a third-year student of the Interior Design. It was a small studio in the house of an architect (who was 20 years older than me). After some time of doing practice, I started to work as an assistant. The moment that I remember most is my first day at work, when I had no idea about the realization of the real projects, and she took me to the construction works of the one she was responsible for. Thanks to her, I had the opportunity to see all the stages of the project from my very first days. At that moment I already knew that I want to work as freelance (not in a big office), collaborating with different people. I worked with this architect for two years. Meanwhile, my daughter was born. As the architect had small kids as well, my family situation was not a problem. I could work at home and combine quite well the time for work, studies and the time with my girl. The most stressful for me was when I had to control the construction works, as the workers treated me like 'the young girl who doesn't know anything'. And the most amazing is that after having my daughter, it changed – I usually was going to the construction work check-up with my daughter (not always, but quite often I didn't have the possibility to have some help of my husband or my parents) and the indirect comments stopped. During the collaboration with this architect, I also started to make projects with my friend from studies or on my own.

e) About the current situation of your professional activities: What opinion do you have about it, have you imagined your future doing exactly what you are doing now, how did you benefit from your cultural and personal legacy, how does the political, economic and cultural background affect you at the moment?

Now I have 5 years of professional experience. While in Poland, I had no problem in getting new projects (normally because of the recommendations of the clients). After my moving to Spain, situation changed a lot. I couldn't get new interior projects, I didn't know anyone here. I started to participate in various competitions – and most of them were successful. I also took part in some work

© Agata Dzianach

shops and started to collaborate with the architectural magazines. And then the topic 'Consciousness of the city' appeared and I devoted myself to that topic and even till this day I continue developing various projects related to it. The crisis in Spain (in Poland our profession doesn't suffer that much, there is no crisis in this field) changed my professional way, but now I see it as a 'plus'. Although I hope I will be able to come back to the interior design projects, I am sure I will develop them simultaneously with the ones related with the city.

f) About other non-paid complementary activities: how do they relate to your current work, what advantages and disadvantages do they generate, in what way do they influence your point of view?

My professional non-paid activities are related to the consciousness of the city and my projects about this topic. It seems to me a very interesting topic which is worth to be done voluntarily. Now I am also a member of the 'Laboratorio de Ideas' (the Ideas' Lab) – a debate platform dedicated to stimulate alternative suggestions in the life of an architect. I work as one of the moderators of the topic 'Different ways to build the city'.

g) About the compatibility between different kinds of activities: How do you achieve it, does it generate any problem or the advantage for you?

After two years being a mother, working and studying at the same time, now I am a mother who works freelance at home. The freelance mode of my work gives me the opportunity of a great flexibility. In many cases, I see it as positive thing, but sometimes I also feel a little bit over-charged. Here, in Spain, there are just three of us, without families, so we are doing everything all together. I am carrying out various projects in different European countries – most of them in distance + some short necessary trips. Despite these business trips, most of which I go to alone, we travel a lot all three of us. Thanks to my way of work, it's quite easy to find the time for the family trips.

h) About the visibility and recognition of your work and other non-paid activities: Do you feel well compensated for your efforts and professional capacity, do you consider you have equal opportunities, or do you have to choose?

Talking about the paid work, I feel well compensated – most of all because of the opinion of my clients (which I consider the most important factor, because I work for people and not for the nice interior picture), since I always get new projects because of their recommendations. I don't expect much more than the user's satisfaction of the spaces I made.

i) About the social point of view of the work made by women: Do you consider the behaviour as fair, do you share your responsibilities with your familiars and/or partners, do you find the language used around you to be discriminatory?

I get a lot of support of my husband and all my family. Working freelance at home I don't feel that I have to choose between my family and work, I feel understood most of the time. I think we have equilibrated everything really well and I feel quite comfortable with my work.

k) About the existence of 'different way of seeing the architecture': Do you consider that there are different points of view, what is your opinion about it, do you think it is positive to insist at this particular point?

What I could say about this topic is that in my opinion architecture is not just a building. Some time ago I realized how important the future users of my project are. I don't admit the architecture as only the nice image. I believe it is something deeper. I notice that many of my friends architects devote themselves only to the building itself without doing something out of the traditional homework. In my opinion architects should spend more time with the people, integrated to the society and not separated as the professionals. Times are changing and I think architecture, as a profession, should be rethought as well, with a goal to serve the people.

l) About the possible prognosis of the near future: How do you see the professional situation in short/long terms, how do you see the social situation of women in short/long terms, do you see any alternatives in professional work of the architects?

I think that both women and men should be more integrated in the society. If opposite, we will have more and more buildings/cities which will not respond to the real necessities. I believe it is a big field to explore. In my opinion this part of the work can seem easier for the women, as I consider them more multidisciplinary in the 'way of exit'. However I also think that a woman can make all of the phases of the project and I would like to avoid the division: work for a woman and work for a man. Maybe it is also the question of understanding the basic thing: that we as women do not need to (and do not have to) have the same way of working and the project process as a man (which for example include the time division for work and for family) – it is a case to explain and make clear to everybody and I feel that the comparison of this kind of issue should be stopped. Only the final result should be highlighted.

© Agata Dzianach

Marilda Azulay Tapiero

D. MARILDA AZULAY TAPIERO, VALENCIA, SPAIN

a) About the current personal and/or family situation: the architect will tell us what she considers relevant about the current situation.

I am 53 years old. I live and work in Valencia. And I am a married women with two kids. I think the same as Emmanuel Levinas wrote, 'I don't have a son; I am, in a particular way, my son'. So if we see it from this perspective, I am, in that particular way, Sarah and Ari, 21 and 17 years old... Being Sarah, I am now in Jerusalem, in the Hebrew University, Bezalel School of Art; being Ari – I study in the French Lyceum of Valencia, and hopefully in two years will be studying in France – adolescence and rugby, for example, also have a lot of importance in my life. I am also an architect, doctor in architecture, professor and investigator.

b) About the point of view of the architecture before the studies: memories of the architectural experiences before the studies started, the point of view at that time (Thinking Architecture, Zumthor).

There are many images and even feelings, coming from my childhood, which are related to the architecture and which were the ones to have the most influence in my formation and, I think, later reflections and works as an architect. It shouldn't look strange, as my life is surrounded by the architecture.

My first images come from the place I was born, Casablanca. Despite the fact that I had to leave this city being five years old, I have it always present in my life. I remember the sea from it, or maybe its encounter with the ocean from the high point of 'The Coast'. I also remember its gardens, contrasting with the white of the buildings.

There are two main spaces from my home in Casablanca that often come to my mind: the kitchen with benches and furniture at each side and a courtyard at the end;

and the balcony hanging over the street, that had a really high parapet with a small protected hole by the ground, through which I could see the street full of people moving around, the terraces of the cafés and etc.

Since the winter of 1963, already in Valencia, my memories are concentrated to a semi-detached apartment block, very simple but vast and full of light. In the first days these memories come as a view of an empty apartment, without any furniture, just a simple wooden staircase which was used as a table and a chair at the same time. Soon, the furniture came, light, modest and comfortable one...[...]

Other place, which impressed me with its architecture, was my school – although I had no idea about it yet. It was the school of Jesús-María which had glazed and clean classrooms, full of light. And a huge courtyard as well, with its sport fields, small pond... and the spiral staircase which impressed me for its shape, size and inexplicable capacity to organize all the entrances from the wide and sunny corridors to the classrooms for so many students at the same moment.

In that time I also started to notice the necessary details lacking in my apartment block: bathroom on the ground floor, light in the staircase, cold in the corridor, long waits for the elevator... or the showers after the sports activities in the school... I have noticed all of it, and was always thinking how I could change it, what it would be like.

c) About the formation as an architect: How did the years of the studies go, what topics/assignments/circumstances had the most influence on your motivation for studies, what do you think now about that period of life, what would you change and what not, what was the political, economic and cultural background at that moment?

I started to study architecture in 1975 – a very important year for the history of Spain – and got the title in 1981. It was the first year or the new plan in which the degree lasted 6 years, and during those six years we moved from one building to another. First of all, we started our studies in the building of the School of Agronomists, which was situated in the campus of Blasco Ibáñez, known as 'live' or 'animated', combining with some practices in the Escuela de Aparejadores, situated in the 'far away' campus in the road of Vera. This last building was also the one in which we had to stay during our second course. I actually enjoyed much more my third and fourth year, as we had classes in one building on the Square of Galicia, as it was situated near Alameda and it was really a nice place to be. And to pass the last years we were already moved to what is now the School of Architecture in the road of Vera.

Despite the professors, few of whom have inspired me-as they were not that enthusiastic themselves-, I searched for the inspirations in the movies, books, music... I want to name two movies which were the most important for me at that time: Luchino Visconti's 'The Damned' of 1969, although premiered in Spain in 1975, and 'Blade Runner' of Ridley Scott in 1982. I was reading Kafka, Asimov, Camus, García Márquez, Borges...; listening to Woody Guthrie, Bob Dylan, Joan Baez, Leonard Cohen, Moustaki ... and Ella Fitzgerald. The 'cultural background' was different, the one called '80's movement'. Although the political moment was more like of the 'illusions', agreements, coexistence, compromises and promises... [...]

d) About the beginning of the professional activities: what did you choose to do in that moment, what influence did this choice had to your current work, what problems/advantages did it generated, what was the political, economic and cultural background at that moment?

I started working being 23 years old. I remember my beginning of the professional collaboration in one architectural studio, considered as 'important' one at the moment; although some months later I understood that this was not what interested me most in architecture.

I had a degree in the 'Building Construction' specialty, and continued later with the Master in Urbanism and courses of Doctorate.

This activity first of all combined with reforms, small single-family housing projects, legalizations, informs... and some competitions, some of which were successful. It was a complex beginning, but happy one. The difficulty was not in developing or elaboration the possible projects, capacity for work, recognition or remuneration, but mostly in its execution, as nobody then believed in the female architect of 23, 24, 25,... years (when it was a time for collaborations, there were only men, hardly someone addressed me in the construction works).

It had to be around 1983 when I met José Luis Ros, the architect and at that time professor of the Elements of Composition in the School. I collaborated with him in some important projects, and we worked in his studio, which with time started to feel as mine as well; it was a really cozy studio, in the centre of the city, always surrounded by the friends... [...]

Teaching (since 1988) and firstly Sarah (1990) and then Ari (1995), without realizing it, have been decanting my professional activity. As well as the elaboration of my doctoral thesis.

e) About the current situation of your professional activities: What opinion do you have about it, have you imagined your future doing exactly what you are doing now, how did you benefit your cultural and personal legacy, how does the political, economic and cultural background affect you at the moment?
Teaching and investigations are the activities to which I dedicate most of my time today, meanwhile still trying to continue with the professional practice: small projects, competitions, collaborations...

I have never expected more than simply satisfying my own needs, for making and saying the things that I consider being right making and saying, and satisfying as well the needs of my past and present students of the department of architectural design. Making projects, and teaching how to do it, I see as a great responsibility which requires maturity and reflection. These qualities are also necessary while dealing with the complexity and high quantity of elements which have to be arranged, coordinated and synthesized by the architect in connection with culture, society, science, industry, history, nature... which are not particularly architectural and not always in the same field. That's why I try to always stay alert and at the same time I trust in participatory, trans-disciplinary, multiple-focal processes; and I tend to guide my investigations towards them. [...]

f) About other not-paid complementary activities: how do they relate with your current work, what advantages and disadvantages do they generate, in what way do they influence your point of view?
Non-paid activities 'economically', which I dedicate a lot of time and attention, give me so many satisfaction as those which are remunerated. It is more, sometimes those activities cost me some money... Some of them are part of my professional activity and formation: studies, investigations, publications, participation and assistance to congresses... Others, because of my own way of being (I refer to 'I *become* through my relation to the *Thou;* as I *become* I', Martin Buber), I conduct them fundamentally towards the fight against the intolerance, the racism, the anti-Semitism, the xenophobia... And it means to respect, to know, to want to know, to announce... I collaborate or have collaborated with diverse institutions, civic and religious associations, cultural centres, with the Movement against the Intolerance, with the Three Religions Chair of the Universitat de València, with different departments of the same university, with diverse school centres... and I try to help to all the calls that I can: always I try to answer yes and to involve as many persons that I can.

Conferences, classes, publications, meetings ... to prepare, to investigate ... that occupy a lot of time, which is remunerated in gratitude, friendship, respect, knowledge... education. And I think that, being formed, also helps me as an architect, helping myself to respect, perceive and understand the reality from different points of view.

j) About the incorporation of the gender perspective to the everyday life: Do you consider that it is necessary to intensify collective incorporation of the gender perspective, do you think that this particular action would bring any improvement (or not), please describe in what way it would affect you?

The image of the reality itself can vary between various observers; because perceiving not only depends on our visual field, point of view, our eyes' health and visual device: the perception of the space is established by the complex process which contains many variables, like memory, memories and experiences, knowledge, information, education, analogues...

I would prefer to talk about the perception (collective, group, individual... of the kids, elderly, women, immigrants, different cultures...) of the space intended to orientate, to live in and to act, be. By all means, urban and architectural scenery perform a social role. [...]

k) About the existence of 'different way of seeing the architecture': Do you consider that there are different points of view, what is your opinion about it, do you think it is positive to insist at this particular point?

[...] I consider fundamental viewing architecture as a subject which together with an object forms part of all, determining each other. (I am coming back to my childhood images). It's a resourceful relationship where each one is modifying the environment and, at the same time, sees it transformed together with its own existence. It requires visibility of the complex systems, interactions and retroactions between the parts and a whole, of the multidimensional entities and of the ESSENTIAL PROBLEMS.

On the other hand, perhaps, like Edgar Morin says, 'There is an increasing, deep and serious lack of adequacy, between our discordant knowledges, cut up into pieces, classified in disciplines and, on the other hand, realities or problems which are more multidisciplinary, transverse, multidimensional, transnational, global and planetary'.

At the same time, he expresses that the weakening of the global perception leads to the weakening of the RESPONSIBILITY: 'Each one tends not to be a person in charge any more than of his specialized tasks', as well as the weakening of the SOLIDARITY, 'Because nobody perceives one's organic tie with one's city and with one's fellow-citizens'.

© Marilda Azulay Tapiero

Inés Novella

E. INÉS NOVELLA, VALENCIA, SPAIN

a) About the actual personal and/or family situation: The architect will tell us what she considers relevant about the actual situation.

Well, since I finished my architecture studies, in September of 2008, my professional situation was always marked by the crisis, as well as my boyfriend's who is also an architect and finished his studies some months later than I did. This is the reason which mostly determines our lives and limits our possibilities. At the moment, after long and tiring searches, we both have jobs which are more or less related to architecture. In my case, I am now a freelance architect and it is just because I haven't got another chance, although in this situation I am trying to get some advantages of being independent and make my job more diverse. I combine my part time job in an architecture studio with the work as a specialized translator of the architectural and engineering texts; at the same time collaborating in teaching and investigating on my own in the field of Equality, the part that interests me most (although I need all the rest to be able to earn money for living) [...]

b) About the point of view of the architecture before the studies: memories of the architectural experiences before the studies started, the point of view at that time (Thinking Architecture, Zumthor).

In that moment, I had no idea what was the architecture and what being an architect meant. And I have no problem to say that if I would have known it, I probably haven't even had started studying architecture in the first place. In my opinion there is a big difference between loving architecture as it is and wishing to become an architect and I think that very few people know this before starting architecture studies, even during university years. I remember that at high school I heard my history-of-art teacher talking about Le Corbusier, and then I thought that I already understood what architecture was [...]

c) About the formation as an architect: How did the years of the studies go, what topics/assignments/ circumstances had the most influence on your motivation for studies, what do you think now about that period of life, what would you change and what not, what was the political, economic and cultural background at that moment?

I started at the School of Architecture in 1999/2000 and finished in 2007/2008; and in these 8 years there were many changes everywhere. When I started my studies, and during many years later (I would say that almost till the last year), the profession was 'going well': as a student I didn't hear anything about unemployment, just some fairytales about possibilities to gain money even while studying in some construction works and etc. And every time you said you were an architecture student, people would adore you (seeing you as a half-god and believing that you are a genius in drawing) or look at you with that strange look (considering that many architects they know are cocky and arrogant). All of this happened in the time of the 'star-architects', big international projects and recognition of the Spanish architecture inside and outside of the country. [...]

I find necessary to mention my Erasmus experience, too, in 2005/2006 in Estonia, because it was a point of a change in my life, both professionally and personally. By chance, I studied there an Urban Studies Master and there I met its new director, Panu Lehtovouri. He was an architect, but he told me a lot about Manuel Castells, Jane Jacobs, Henry Lefevre... and I had a lot of classmates who were geographers, landscape designers, economists... We had classes with Hille Koskela, who was the first person to talk to me about the differential reality between the fact of being a woman or a man, and how it conditions the way one uses the city. At that time I really understood so little... Where I came from, I was used to give all my efforts to pass the technical assignments of the course, to calculate rebars, to think about the constructive details at a scale 1:5... and to understand urbanism as a geometri-

cal composition more than anything else. I learned a lot in Tallinn, and I think it was there where I unconsciously started to walk towards issues that I now consider as the most important ones; and most of all, there I widened my point of view and revived my vision of architecture and the role of architects in the city planning process.

d) About the beginning of the professional activities: What did you choose to do in that moment, what influence did this choice have to your actual work, what problems/advantages did it generate, what was the political, economic and cultural background at that moment?

The lack of work obliged me to do other things and gave me the opportunity to continue with my studies, firstly doctorate courses at the Department of City Planning (when I didn't have any job at all), and later the Master of Equal of Opportunities, which was held online and allowed me to combine it with my full-time job.

e) About the actual situation of your professional activities: What opinion do you have about it, have you imagined your future doing exactly what you are doing now, how did you benefit from your cultural and personal legacy, how does the political, economic and cultural background affect you at the moment?

I am worried about the profession, and I don't talk about the good or bad architecture that is being made now, I talk about the obsolete labour structure that we have, based on what years ago was consisted to be an architect, when there were just few of them, all of whom were men and mostly the ones from a 'good' social class. Nowadays most of us are workers, without any contract, but workers, and we don't have a labour structure for that. I would say that there are two classes of architects now: the employers and the employees.

f) About other non-paid complementary activities: How do they relate with your actual work, what advantages and disadvantages do they generate, in what way do they influence your point of view?

I would divide my non-paid activities into two groups. Firstly, the voluntary or the active citizenship ones and secondly the ones that are related to the work of care, what sometimes is called 'reproductive work'. Most of my non-paid activities belong to the first group and I can give more time to it because I don't have care and family burdens, otherwise it would be harder. Anyway, the extensive working hours that architects have make it very difficult to balance issues like family/work, or just to be an active citizen. It requires additional efforts.

For that reason during almost all my studying years I was a monitor in my Scout group, later I was a volunteer in Oxfam and now I'm an active member of SOSTRE. I've been adapting this type of activities to each moment of my life to have a better conciliation between my work, studies and non-paid activities.

g) About the compatibility between different kinds of activities: How do you achieve it, does it generate any problem or the advantage for you?
I think I have answered this in the last question. Architects' working dynamics make it more difficult to combine different kinds of activities, and this especially has much more impact on women. I would recommend the last article of Inés S. de Madariaga about this topic.

h) About the visibility and recognition of your work and other non-paid activities: Do you feel well compensated for your efforts and professional capacity, do you consider you have equal opportunities, or do you have to choose?
The non-paid work I've done has never had an instant recognition, but I think it's not something you seek in the first place. Personally it has always been something that has enriched me. As I don't have any family burden, I have more time and freedom for this sort of things, although I don't know if I will be able to continue like this in the future, I will have to adapt it once again.

i) About the social point of view of the work made by women: Do you consider the behaviour as fair, do you share your responsibilities with your familiars and/or partners, do you find the language used around you to be discriminatory?
I don't have a feeling of suffering from a discriminatory language surrounding me, although I have always called myself 'arquitectA' (female architect), I think this is the logic way of calling a woman who practices this profession.

In my opinion the most important is to claim of the work of women, although I don't know if it's alright to call it this way, as there could arise a controversy because many people see the term 'women' as opposite to 'men'. The activities I claim are the ones that traditionally were associated to women because it was mostly women who were in charge of it. But, logically, it would be the same for those men who have done or do this sort of tasks [...]

j) About the incorporation of the gender perspective to the everyday life: Do you consider that it is necessary to intensify collective incorporation of the gender perspective, do you think that this particular action would bring any improvement (or not), please describe in what way it would affect you?
Introducing the gender perspective is fundamental, but it has to be explained very well, it should be clear that by doing it nobody has to lose; nothing has to be stolen from men and given to women. By incorporating this differential reality of the female world, everybody would win in new perspectives to the old problems, new solutions,

© Inés Novella

new ways… just what we most need in the times of crisis. And this is the political spirit of the positive discrimination measure… but this should be explained much better than it is done now, because if not, it becomes counterproductive.

To incorporate the reality of women, their visions, experiences and necessities means to incorporate directly half of the population. And in addition to that, the reality of all those people who are associated to feminine activities, like children, elderly or disabled people, is also incorporated, although not in that direct way. If we talk about the specific field of the architecture and planning, the result would be a built space able to respond to the everyday lives of all citizens, better cities, buildings and houses for each and every one.

k) About the existence of 'different way of seeing the architecture': Do you consider that there are different points of view, what is your opinion about it, do you think it is positive to insist at this particular point?
Women and men are different, and not only physically but also culturally. With time, equal rights of men and women have been achieved and the goal now is the equity of roles and profiles – to give more value to the feminine issues, like we do to masculine ones. It is necessary if we want to make this equality work, to make it effective and real. And here is a lot of work in front of us, first of all didactical one, because there are too many of those who believe that women already have equal conditions just because it is how our constitution or human rights are established. The starting position of the women, comparing to the one of men, is not that evident, and the majority of society doesn't know the obstacles which hinder effective equality. This is the reason why most people think this way, even women themselves. We are all in the same androcentric culture, and it is quite difficult to open the eyes and achieve the new perspective of the reality.

l) About the possible prognosis of the near future: How do you see the professional situation in short/long terms, how do you see the social situation of women in short/long terms, do you see any alternatives in professional work of the architects?
Talking about the short-term, near future, I am not an optimist – the progress of the equality is always decreasing in times of economical crisis, because the public cuts in social issues are mostly absorbed by the contribution of women, whose family and community burdens are increased. It makes the family/work balancing even more difficult, as well as their incorporation to the professional sphere, and finally it all consolidates women professional departures and inequality at work. In the further future, I have to be more optimistic, I believe that society will take a step forward in the field of equality, and not only between men and women. I am totally sure that the incorporation of the gender perspective and the achievement of and equal society is good for everyone, if only for the benefit of it, I believe it will be achieved.

© Inés Novella

Cristina Alonso

F. CRISTINA ALONSO, VALENCIA, SPAIN

a) About the current personal and/or family situation: The architect will tell us what she considers to be more relevant about her current situation.

I married Manuel in December 2003. We have two children: Pablo is 5 years old and María is 4. Manuel (Segarra) is a musician and violinist in the Valencia's Orchestra. Our professional situation allows us to invest time on Pablo and María and to participate, more or less equally, in the domestic and professional lives. One of our priorities are our children, so we always try to make sure that at least one of us will be at home when they come back from school, although we are lucky to have young grandparents who are always keen on giving us a hand.

b) About what you thought before studying the architecture degree: memories of the architectural experiences that you had before the studying architecture, looking at it from a nowadays perspective. (Thinking Architecture, Zumthor).

When I was 6 years old, me and my family moved to Valencia (my father is an engineer and depending on the projects he had to work on, the whole family had to move from one city to another). I was quite upset – it was the first time I was aware about the move – and we stayed with my grandparents while my parents were looking for a place to live and to study in Valencia. When they came back, my dad tried to change my mind by telling me stories of what they had been doing those days in Valencia and he even drew me the plan of the house they have rented. I was fascinated, how well I could see it!

When I was 9, I asked my dad who were the ones who made these plans before the houses were built, and he answered me that these people were called 'architects'. So since then I named what I wanted to be when I grew up. Little by little I started to find out the architecture meanings and its implications and every time I liked more the option I had chosen in my childhood.

c) About your education as an architect: How did the university years go, what topics/subjects/circumstances influenced or motivated you most, what do you think now about that period of your life, what would you have changed and what not, what was the political, economic and cultural atmosphere at that moment?

During the first years of my architectural studies, I got through the subjects without stepping out the officially predefined path for architecture students. Even though, in the fourth course, urbanism professors – Matilde Alonso and Juan Luis Piñón – offered me collaboration with them within the UPV Urbanism Department. What as a set out could have just been a simple collaboration in specific projects, eventually happened to become for me, a whole learning process in parallel to my official academic education. Apart from the projects, I collaborated as a lecturer and we organized a congress about the 'Informal City' in Colombia which was not only an opportunity to get to know other architects who worked in related topics as cities with informal growth, but also a lifetime experience to see the outskirt suburbs of several Colombian cities. It also gave me the opportunity to participate in lectures, publications, proposals, trips, and so on.

All of this work was made by a small group of people (various architects, professors, students ...) which helped me to become an architect, shape my own critical view and gain experience; things that I wouldn't have been able to acquire by simply getting through my degree.Once I finished my studies, I left the University behind and all my professional activities that related with it. Even so, I kept my relation and collaboration with Matilde Alonso, Carmen Blasco and Francisco J. Martinez, while I was working on my Third Degree. This period of my life was very important in terms of my formation. In order to give back my gratitude to all the opportunities I was given, I try to give new chances to students and scholarships holders by participating in the Technical Office of the city council in Meliana (my current work); creating and developing projects related to Meliana's local government.

d) About the beginning of the professional activities: what did you do in that moment, what influence did this choice have on your current work, what problems/advantages did it generate, what was the political, economic and cultural background at that moment?

I finished my studies in October of 2004, which was a time with a high demand in construction. However, it wasn't until February of 2005 that I got the chance to develop in any 'active' project since, after all those years of collaboration with University, I found it hard to dissociate both realities. First of all, due to the doctorate courses I started in the Urbanism Department in UPV and secondly because it was a time of chaos and lack of control in the construction sector and I didn't want to take part of it. Moreover, at that time I was already married to Manuel who had a good job and this allowed me to consider the places I wanted to work in without the need of taking the first one that I was offered.

Maybe due to my curriculum at University or to the fact that there was quite a lot of work in the architectural field, after sending my curriculum to Colegio de Arquitectos I received three calls in a week offering me a job. I finally chose one of them and worked there for two months, combining professional activity with my doctorate in the UPV. After those two months, I got the opportunity to work in the Territory and Housing Local Authority in the specific field of 'territorial organization service and planning of Valencia'. During these years, while I was working in the Public Administration, my economic wage was lower than before and my work became a little bit too bureaucratic compared to what one expects to be the work of an architect. However, I noticed from the very beginning, that this kind of work, directed on society and common interests was the one to fulfil my professional expectations and fully made worth the disadvantages one could see with a quick look.

e) About the actual situation of your professional activities: What opinion do you have about it, have you imagined your future doing exactly what you are doing now, how did you benefit from your cultural and personal legacy, how does the political, economic and cultural background affect you at the moment?

After two years in the Territory and Housing Local Authority, I had been working for almost two years more in the City Council of Godella – the place where I discovered the other side of the Public Administration – and after which I returned to my job in the Territory and Housing Local Authority (this time to the General Direction of the Landscape). My job in Godella didn't last long, just two months, because I was chosen as a municipal architect of the City Council of Meliana, where I have been working for already three years.

The professional period that I am living right now is really special and exciting for me, first of all because my work is highly valued and also because many initiatives and priorities, planted in the Technical Office, are being accepted and developed. For example, we are now making the Edition of the General Plan of the Urban Organization, led by the City Council itself; our plans of restoration of 'Palau Nolla' are initializing, etc. And as a matter of fact, the economic situation right now makes possible important changes in the municipality without the pressure of possible urban planners and sponsors.

f) About other non-profit complementary activities: hHw do they relate with your current work, what advantages and disadvantages do they generate, in what way do they influence your point of view?

As a consequence of the Academic formation in the third cycle of my doctorate program 'The city, territory and landscape in the period of globalization' in the Department of Urbanism in UPV, I have focused my investigations in the relationship between cities and their surroundings, and in particular project of the growth of the urban spaces of L'Horta Nord and its fertile region. I had

started this investigation before any other professional activity, and in spite of this, the places that I have been working in happened to relate in a very close way to this academic investigation and my professional work.

On the other hand, my membership in the associations not related to the architecture and participation in various social voluntary events had widened my point of view and my global vision of the world, which generally is quite limited as we are used to move around in only one particular social background.

A non-profit Spanish organization, 'El Parto es Nuestro', consists of the users and professionals who have a goal to improve the conditions and provide necessary attention for mothers and their children during the pregnancy, as well as after and before it. When I to join the Association which I found already after of my own pregnancy. And I can assure that the participation in this association has opened to me a surprisingly new world of the gender perspective.

g) About the compatibility between different kinds of activities: How do you achieve it, does it generate any problem or the advantage for you?

I consider that the main problem of combining different activities is their lack of flexibility in terms of time. In my case, my husband is the main and essential reason for my daily schedule, activities and their timing. We share our daily duties in a more or less balanced way, as well as the vision of how to raise Pablo and María. Whenever I feel I need any help revising texts, he is always there to help me. In fact, despite of having totally different professions, we succeed to combine them quite well. This compatibility of our common life benefits us in a way so that we can develop both professionally and personally. On the other hand, as I have mentioned before, my professional interests relates well with my employment, and this is one of the keys to be able to combine these two sides of my life.

h) About the recognition of your work and other non-paid activities: Do you feel well compensated for your efforts and professional capacity, do you consider you have equal opportunities, or did you have to choose?

At the moment I do feel that my work is highly valued, and what is more, my necessities in both personal and family conditions are respected and understood. This leads to the fact that the motivation for my work is even higher than it would be in normal conditions. Besides, I feel that I have the same rights as I would if I were a man.

However, there also have been moments when I have experienced some kind of mobbing – although they did not point out at me personally, but the entire department – eventually, the one who had to leave was me. And exactly the day when I gave birth to my daughter (and taking advantage of this circumstance) that they decided to use this day for the negotiations with the labour unions about the temporary staff.

But talking about the non-profit activities, in my opinion, sometimes it's hard to have commitments, as my family is always my first priority.

i) About the social point of view of the work made by women: Do you consider the behaviour fair distributed? Do you share your responsibilities with your familiars and/or partners, do you find a 'discriminatory language' around you?

Practically all the time, I feel being treated in a right and correct way. Although there were times, mostly because of older and 'old-school' architects, when I felt a little bit discriminated in two aspects: firstly for being a female and secondly for being young. They come to me to ask for a consultation but when they see me, they don't even ask any questions, just start to teach me how I should complete their files and I even have to listen them calling me 'well, bonica'... But it is true, it only happened few times. However, I have never felt any discrimination or underestimation from my co-workers, neither because of my work, nor for any other personal or family related reason. Even the opposite, I have always felt highly valued and well treated (exactly the same way as my male co-workers).

URBANISMO Y PAISAJE
09/10   MELIANA

© Cristina Alonso

G. LOLA DOMÈNECH, BARCELONA, SPAIN

Lola Domènech

b) About the point of view of the architecture before the studies: memories of the architectural experiences before the studies started, the point of view at that time (Thinking Architecture, Zumthor).

My childhood memories, as long as I can remember them, are that drawing was one of my particular refugees on Sunday mornings. Some games from the times I was still a kid come to my mind: the construction of the temporal hut situated near the river which we built with discovery and exploration of an old abandoned mansion in my home town, which we found during one summer and it was something that excited me so much…

These first and maybe unconscious steps probably were those which finally determined my future passion for the architecture.

c) About the formation as an architect: How did the years of the studies go, what topics/assignments/circumstances had the most influence on your motivation for studies, what do you think now about that period of life, what would you change and what not, what was the political, economic and cultural background at that moment?

I remember my time in the School of Architecture of Barcelona as a really nice moment of my life. The first year of the studies was a little bit of suffering, first of all because there were no classes such as architectural design, and the ones that were most interesting of all were drawing and history of architecture. Anyway, from the second course year everything changed quite pleasingly. At that time the whole architecture degree lasted six years plus the final project. So the second year was the one when we were introduced to the world of designing and creating architecture. And it was this time when I started to feel my chosen carrier in a global sense. In this first year of designing I had much luck to be taught by wonderful professors, such as Enric Miralles who worked at the chair held by Federico Correa. Miralles was a very passionate and devoted architect and transmitted these qualities and emotions very well to all the students. Being in his classes was a real excitement. My first projects in the school were recognized and appreciated really well and further development of the architectural designing was a profitable process led by never ending growth and progress of the ideas. In later courses I had the luck to get to know the professors, such as Elias Torres, Yago Conde, Manuel Brullet, Manuel de Solà Morales, Quim Español, Albert Viaplana, Helio Piñón...

The period of studies was also a period of various architectural trips in which we, the small group of students, got familiarized and influenced by all the architecture we had the opportunity to pass by: Le Corbusier, Álvaro Siza, Foster, Adolf Loos, Alvar Aalto...

d) About the beginning of the professional activities: What did you choose to do in that moment, what influence did this choice have on your current work, what problems/advantages did it generate, what was the political, economic and cultural background at that moment? During my studies in the university and the first years of professional activities (since year 1996), I collaborated in various studios with the architects like LLuís Cantallops, Yago Conde, Josep LLuís Mateo, Joan Busquests... In the end of my studies I had the opportunity to collaborate as well in the Department of the Urban Projects in the City Council of Barcelona, and it was a place where for the first time I established a contact with a design and planning of the public space. Since this first experience I started to relate my works more directly with urban planning and intervention in the landscape. I finished my studies in ETSAB in the year 1992. And this was the post-Olympic time right then, time full of difficulties. The period previous to Olympic Games in Barcelona was really beneficial one, but from the time it finished, many architects faced unemployment and it got really difficult for young ones to open their path towards the profession. I remember

my first years of professional collaboration with other architects, years when I was also devoted to my own studio (since 1996, together with my partner Quim Rosell at that moment). In these first years we mostly participated in various competitions which finally brought us recognition and first prizes.

It was a difficult start, but our enthusiasm and insistence left behind all the difficulties of that particular moment.

e) About the current situation of your professional activities: What opinion do you have about it, have you imagined your future doing exactly what you are doing now, how did you benefit from your cultural and personal legacy, how does the political, economic and cultural background affect you at the moment? My professional path during these 16 years was mostly based on constancy and persistence together with the never-ending search of new ways towards brave and understandable architecture. This chosen path is far from 'easily-built' architecture, I didn't pretend to follow fashionable or accustomed guidelines in any way. At times like now, specified by the lack of common sense and loss of universal values, we should fight and preserve the dignity of the architecture. The architecture forms a big part of our culture and we must protect it from the manipulation and lack of criteria. Like José Luís Sampedro, writer and economist, once said, we can't build our world based only on economics. There are a lot of other great values, less ephemeral and much more solid and stable, which ones we should recover, recreate and resituate. The economic value usually becomes instant and temporal.

From our personal position we should always work thinking about how to preserve the architecture from all the speculative or economic manipulation. This architecture should be connected with its socioeconomic and environmental background and at the same time be in search of a new possibilities. My current professional

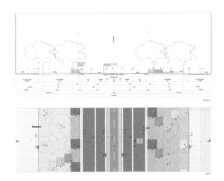

© Lola Domènech

activities center on my own studio and classes that I give for the Master of Interiors called 'Private Perimeters' which takes place in the school Elisava (related to the University of Pompeu Fabra).

j) About the incorporation of the gender perspective to the everyday life: Do you consider that it is necessary to intensify collective incorporation of the gender perspective, do you think that this particular action would bring any improvement (or not), please describe in what way it would affect you?
It is obvious that there is still a long way to go towards a change in this particular aspect. However, I think that our generation and the one that follows have resolved much better the ideas of gender. Despite this fact, we still carry along the problem of the proceeding generations as well as the incorporation of the women in some professional areas, which also includes architecture.

k) About the existence of 'different way of seeing the architecture': Do you consider that there are different points of view, what is your opinion about it, do you think it is positive to insist at this particular point?
I think that it is neither healthy nor positive insisting in this point just because the difference, which in my opinion is far from important, gets bigger and bigger; like when I read some book or see the piece of art, I value it by the emotions that it provokes, leaving behind the consideration of the gender that it could generate.

l) About the possible prognosis of the near future: How do you see the professional situation in short/long terms, how do you see the social situation of women in short/long terms, do you see any alternatives in professional work of the architects?
I am very sad to see that each time more and more projects are based on exaggeration of conflicting with each other and the architects find themselves navigating in this sea of obstacles. And this excess of incompatible regulations and bureaucracy in my opinion just decreases

the quality of the architecture. The process of any designing nowadays is too much restricted by the excessive regulations. The good architecture should escape this and give a new and obstacle-free response to the rigidity of what is pre-established.

m) About any other specific topic that you would like to debate and/or describe us your point of view.
I am especially interested in the individual and risky architecture, which has been created to a specific place. I admire the architecture which explores the surroundings and looks forward as well as takes into count the past experiences. I trust without any doubt in looking backwards to make a step forward.

On the other hand, I am irritated by the architecture which calls itself 'green', sustainable, eco-efficient or environmentally integrated. The good architecture was always controlled by the basic concepts of efficiency, sustainability and integration to the landscape. And it doesn't need a mask to hide behind these labels which usually work only with newly applied technologies, leaving behind the basic criteria of the passive yet wise architecture.

n) About the personal considerations you would like to highlight: Is there anything else you would like to share with us?
In their everyday work architects have a responsibility to offer and defend great and authentic models of architecture which are always in search for a new ways. Architects should be able to create new atmospheres, like Peter Zumthor explains in his book called 'Atmospheres'. And for the final word I would like to share the short poem of Mario Benedetti: 'The simplicity is the most complex power'.

© Lola Domènech

WIEN VIENNA

On Stage! Wien, Stop 2014

Doris Damyanovic, Aurélie Karlinger
Gesa Witthöft, Petra Hirschler

„In Szene setzen – On Stage!" lautete das Motto der Studentinnen von der BOKU und TU Wien, die Frauen aus der feministischen und genderspezifischen Planung im Rahmen der gemeinsamen Lehrveranstaltung „Gender- und Diversity-Aspekte in Planung und Berufsleben" im Wintersemester 2013/2014 porträtierten.

An der BOKU hat die Auseinandersetzung mit gendersensiblen Inhalten in den Planungswissenschaften ihren Ursprung in den 1980er Jahren. Seitdem berücksichtigt die BOKU feministische und gendersensitive Aspekte in Forschung und Lehre in der Landschaftsplanung und Landschaftsarchitektur. Auch in der Fakultät Architektur und Raumplanung an der TU Wien haben feministische und gendersensitive Aspekte, Dimensionen und Inhalte, begünstigt durch die deutliche anwendungs- und gesellschaftsorientierte Ausrichtung dieser Disziplinen, seit Ende der 1980er Jahre Eingang in Forschung und Lehre gefunden.

In Wien war einerseits das Sichtbarmachen von Frauen und Genderexpertinnen so wichtig, weil das Wirken und Können von Fachfrauen und gendersensitiven KollegInnen – trotz aller Implementierungserfolge in formaler, inhaltlicher und institutioneller Hinsicht – unseres Erachtens noch lange nicht im Mainstream angekommen sind. Ohne Sichtbarkeit aber kann die weitere Verbreitung frauenbezogener, feministischer, gender- und diversitätssensitiver, und damit immer qualitätsverbessernder, Prozesse und Projekte, gerade unter den derzeitig gegebenen finanziellen Bedingungen und einem möglicherweise drohenden gesellschaftspolitischen Backlash, nur schwer befördert werden. Andererseits erfolgte im Seminar auch eine Auseinandersetzung mit gendersensitiven Ansätzen in der Planung durch die ausgewählten Expertinnen. Der gendersensitive Ansatz bezeichnet mehr als ein konkretes Planungskonzept.

Er ist vielmehr ein integrativer Ansatz in den Planungsdisziplinen, der sowohl forschungsstrategisch-programmatische als auch methodologische, methodische und inhaltliche Dimensionen beinhaltet (DAMYANOVIC und ZIBELL, 2013). Grundlage dieses derzeit in Theorie und Praxis weitgehend geteilten Zugangs ist ein intersektionales Verständnis; das heißt die Integration verschiedener Lebenswirklichkeiten, Perspektiven und Interessenslagen von Menschen bezogen auf das biologische wie soziale Geschlecht in der systematischen Zusammenführung mit anderen gesellschaftsbildenden Kategorien wie Alter, Lebenssituation, ethnischen, kulturellen und sozialen Hintergründen und in Bezug auf gesellschaftliche Strukturierungs- und Handlungspraktiken (QUING, 2011). Daher zielt genderspezifische Planung darauf ab, genderspezifische Aspekte in allen Schritten und in allen Handlungsfeldern des Planungsprozesses zu integrieren: von der Formulierung der Ziele und Inhalte über den Planungsprozess und die Implementierung von Maßnahmen bis zur Evaluierung.

Im Gegensatz zu den vorhergehenden Konzepten von Hannover und Valencia, wo hauptsächlich Porträts von Architektinnen für die Ausstellung erarbeitet wurden, war es der Wunsch für die Ausstellung in Wien, Porträts von in Österreich tätigen Frauen aus dem breiteren Feld der Planung, insbesondere auch aus dem Bereich der Landschaftsplanung, zu erarbeiten und zeigen.

Der nächste Schritt galt demnach der Erarbeitung eines eigenen Ausstellungskonzeptes für Wien. Als Ausgangspunkt dienten zur Erstellung die Erfahrungen aus den vorangegangenen Ausstellungen. An dieser Stelle ist zu erwähnen, dass die Lehrveranstaltung in Wien unter anderem auch durch einen Gastbeitrag von Eva Álvarez bereichert wurde.

Am Beginn standen vor allem viele Fragen. Was ist das Ziel der Ausstellung? Was soll vermittelt werden? Wer ist die Zielgruppe? Wer sind die Interviewpartnerinnen? Wie werden die Interviews geführt? Wie sollen die Frauen porträtiert werden?

On Stage! Vienna, Stop 2014

Doris Damyanovic, Aurélie Karlinger
Gesa Witthöft, Petra Hirschler

'Set the scene – ON STAGE!' had been the slogan by the students presenting portraits of women in feminist and gender-specific planning as part of the joint course 'Gender and Diversity Aspects in Planning and Practice' at the BOKU and TU Vienna during the winter term 2013/2014. At the BOKU, discussion of gender-sensitive content in the planning sciences originated in the 1980s. Since then, the BOKU has taken into account feminist and gender-sensitive aspects in research and teaching in landscape planning and landscape architecture. Feminist and gender-sensitive aspects, dimensions and content, supported by the clear application and society-oriented focus of these disciplines, have also been included in research and teaching in the Faculty of Architecture and Spatial Planning at the TU Vienna since the end of the 1980s.

On the one hand, making women and gender experts visible was so important in Vienna, because the activities, skills and knowledge of female experts and gender-sensitive colleagues are, in our opinion, still far from being part of the mainstream – despite all the successes in implementation, in formal, content and institutional terms. Without visibility however, the further spread of women-specific, feminist, gender and diversity-sensitive processes and projects, the quality of which is constantly improving, is difficult to promote, especially under the existing financial conditions and the threat of what may be a socio-political backlash.

On the other hand, through the selected female experts also discussion on gender-sensitive approaches in planning took place in the seminar. The gender-sensitive approach is much more than one specific planning concept. It is, rather, an integral approach to planning disciplines, containing both research-strategy and programmatic, methodological, methodical and content-related dimensions (DAMYANOVIC and ZIBELL, 2013). The basis of this approach, currently largely divided into theory and practice, is an intersectional understanding; thus, the integration of various life realities, prospects and interests of people in terms of biological and social gender in systematic combination with other society-building categories such as age, life situation, ethnic, cultural and social backgrounds, and in relation to every day practices and practices of social structuring (QUING, 2011). Therefore, gender-specific planning aims at integrating gender-specific aspects at all stages and in all spheres of the planning process: from the formulation of objectives and contents, via the planning process and the implementation of measures, up to the evaluation. In contrast to the previous concepts of Hanover and Valencia, where mainly portraits of female architects were developed for the exhibitions, it was the desire for the Viennese exhibition, to develop and show portraits of women working in Austria from the broader field of planning, in particular including the sphere of landscape planning.

The next step therefore had to be the development of a separate exhibition concept for Vienna. Experiences from the previous exhibitions however served as an outset for the development. At this point it is worth to mention that the courses in Vienna were accompanied and enriched by a guest contribution from Eva Álvarez.

At the inception stood many unanswered questions. What is the objective of the exhibition? What is it intended to convey? Who is the target group? Who are the interview partners? How will the interviews be conducted? How will the women be portrayed? From what content will the portraits be compiled? What materials will be needed?

These questions gave rise to further questions, resulting in turn in sets of themes upon which the students would subsequently form working groups. This was how the concept and the exhibition itself gradually took shape.

As subsequently emerged from the concept – the aim of the exhibition was to discuss why gender mainstreaming and diversity are important in planning and which person-

Aus welchen Inhalten werden die Porträts zusammengestellt? Welche Materialien werden benötigt?

Aus diesen Fragen ergaben sich weitere Fragen, aus denen sich wiederum Themenblöcke ergaben, zu denen die Studentinnen im späteren Verlauf Arbeitsgruppen bildeten. So gewann das Konzept, wie auch die Ausstellung selbst, nach und nach an Form.

Ziel der Ausstellung war es – wie später aus dem Konzept hervorging –, zu erörtern, warum Gender Mainstreaming und Diversity in der Planung wichtig sind und welche persönlichen Motivationen dazu führen, in diesem Bereich zu arbeiten. Hauptfokus der Ausstellung war es, Einzelpersonen, genauer: Frauen aus dem Arbeitsfeld der Planung, anhand von gesammelten Informationen – durch mit ihnen geführte Interviews – zu porträtieren und in den Vordergrund, sprich „auf die Bühne" = „On Stage" zu stellen. Bei der Auswahl der Interviewpartnerinnen ging es den Studentinnen darum, eine Bandbreite vieler Bereiche zu zeigen, in welchen Frauen – innerhalb und angelehnt an die Disziplin der Planung – tätig sind und in der Umsetzung der Porträts, deren persönliche und gesellschaftliche Wertvorstellungen, sowie vor allem ihr individuelles Engagement im Berufsleben als auch im Privatleben zu zeigen. In der Breite war es ihnen ein Anliegen, ausgehend von der Planung, auch deren Bezüge zur Politik, Wissenschaft, Bildung, Wirtschaft und Verwaltung mit einzubeziehen. Aufgrund der starken Vernetztheit dieser einzelnen Sparten erschien es ihnen von Bedeutung, die Vielfalt an Arbeitsbereichen und auch die Art und Weisen, wie sich diese mit Gender Mainstreaming und Diversity auseinandersetzen, in die Ausstellung mit einfließen zu lassen. Ein besonderes Anliegen war ihnen dabei, die Beweggründe und die Motivation zur Arbeit mit Gender Mainstreaming zu erfragen und zu porträtieren. Während sie an privaten Hintergründen insbesondere die persönliche Motivation in Bezug zum Thema Gender Mainstreaming im individuellen Alltag und das Verständnis dessen interessierte, sollten mit der beruflichen Tätigkeit der Werdegang, persönliche Erfahrungen in Arbeits-

verhältnissen und Gender Mainstreaming-bezogene Projekte dargestellt werden.

Wichtig war es den Studentinnen, ebenso eine große Vielfalt an – nicht in die Ausstellung involvierten – Personen anzusprechen. Dies sollte eine Möglichkeit darstellen, auch Personen, welche wenig mit Planung im humanwissenschaftlichen Kontext zu tun haben, die Bedeutung von Gender Mainstreaming für unsere Gesellschaft näherzubringen.

Umgesetzt wurde das Konzept in einem dreiteiligen Ausstellungsdesign. Dieses setzte sich aus einem einleitenden Teil zusammen, der zur allgemeinen Information zum Thema diente und Fakten, Definitionen und Begriffserklärungen beinhaltete (Timeline), um eine Einordnung und Kontextualisierung des für Wien erarbeiteten Ausstellungsinhalts zu ermöglichen. Der zweite Teil und Hauptteil der Ausstellung zeigte die Porträts der Frauen mit Betonung auf deren Tätigkeit als Planerinnen und einem Fokus auf deren persönliche Lebenssituation sowie individuellen Werdegang (Plakate). Der dritte Teil umfasste die Vorstellung einzelner Projekte aus dem Tätigkeitsbereich der Frauen – in Form von Projekt-Steckbriefen auf selbstgefertigten Kartonwürfeln – welche sich mit der Gender- und Diversity-Thematik befassten.

Da die Studentinnen den porträtierten Frauen eine „Bühne" geben wollten, haben sie das auch symbolisch mit einer selbstgebauten Bühne für die Ausstellung umgesetzt. Hier wurden die Projekt-Steckbrief-Würfel zu den einzelnen Frauen platziert. Zur Bewerbung der Ausstellung gab es neben Bannern und Plakaten auch ausgewählte Zitate der Frauen aus den Interviews zum Mitnehmen.

Im Sommersemester 2014 wurde das Seminar an der TU Wien angeboten. Die Studierenden arbeiteten ein Ausstellungskonzept für die 8. European Conference of Gender Equality for Higher Education aus.

al motivations lead to work in this field. The main focus of the exhibition was to portray individuals, specifically women from the sphere of planning, using information gathered through personal interviews, and to spotlight them, i.e. give them a 'stage'. Regarding the selection of interview partners, it was important to the students to show a range of spheres in which women work – within and in proximity to the discipline of planning – and to portray their personal values and social moral concepts and in particular to show their individual commitment in professional life as well as in private life. One of their concerns was to include, beyond planning, the women's relationship to politics, science, education, economy and administration of the exhibition. Due to the intense complexity of these individual fields, it seemed important to them to discuss the variety of spheres of work and also the manner in which these deal with gender mainstreaming and diversity. They were particularly keen to inquire about and portray the wide-ranging motives and motivations to work with gender mainstreaming. While they were interested in private backgrounds and personal motivations related to gender mainstreaming in the individual everyday life and its understanding, the professional career activity should portray the development of personal experiences in working situations and gender mainstreaming-related projects.

Furthermore, it was also important to the students to address a wide range of people not involved in the exhibition. This was intended as an opportunity to raise awareness also among people having little to do with planning in a human sciences related context and to convey the significance of gender mainstreaming to our society as a whole.

The concept was implemented in a three-part exhibition design. This consisted of an introductory part serving to provide general information on the issue and containing facts, definitions and explanations of terms (timeline) in order to enable a thematical classification and contextualisation of the exhibition content developed for Vienna. The second and main part of the exhibition showed the portraits of the women, emphasising their activity as planners and with a focus on their personal life situations as well as individual career progression (posters). The third part dealt with the presentation of individual projects from the spheres of activities of the women – in form of project profiles on hand-made cubes – dealing with gender and diversity-related issues.

As the students wanted to give the portrayed women a platform, they also presented this symbolically with a stage they built themselves for the exhibition. On the stage the project cubes to each individual woman were placed. To advertise the exhibition, selected quotations by the women out of the interviews and printed on flyers were given for take away, in addition to the compiled banners and posters.

During the summer term of 2014 the seminar was again proposed at the TU Vienna, forming part of the framework programme for the 8th European Conference of Gender for Higher Education in September 2014. The exhibition was hence shown once again.

REFERENCES

DAMYANOVIC, Doris; ZIBELL, Barbara 2013: Is there still gender on the agenda for spatial planning theories? Attempt to an integrative approach to generate gender-sensitive planning theories. DISP. 49, pp.25–36

QUING. 2011: Advancing Gender+ Training in Theory and Practise. An International Event for Practitioners, Experts and Commissioners in Gender-Training, Madrid

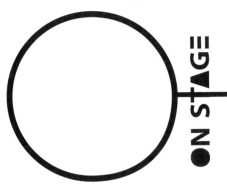

ON ST**A**GE

1900   **1920**

1897

Women were accepted as regular students at the philosophical faculties of the universities of the Austro-Hungarian monarchy. In 1900, the admission of women to medical schools/studies followed. In 1919, women were granted the admission to the University of Veterinary Medicine and to studies of legal and political sciences (PRIMOST, 1968, 2).

1906

Finland is the first European country with women's suffrage, followed by Norway in 1913, Denmark in 1915, Azerbaijan – as first Muslim country – in 1917 and Austria in 1919 (DEUTSCHER BUNDESTAG, 2016).

1914–1918

First World War. It leads to the fall of the German, Ottoman and Austro-Hungarian Empires.

1915

First entry of a female assistant at the faculty for plant breeding (curriculum at the 'k.k. Hochschule für Bodenkultur' – today: University of Natural Resources and Life Sciences, Vienna). Later on, there were further entries regarding temporary female assistants (BAUER, 1927, 21).

1919

Admission for women to technical academies – at the BOKU Vienna initially only to agricultural studies. In 1872, the BOKU Vienna was founded with the sections for agriculture and forestry. There had already been female non-degree students before women were officially admitted to those studies (BAUER, 1927, 20).

1922

Sophie Rumenovic de Jezerane, born on October 28, 1897 in Fiume (nowadays Rijeka/Croatia) passed a regular study at the BOKU Vienna as first female graduate. She had started her studies as non-degree student in winter term 1916/17 and continued from winter term 1919/20 (AUFNAHMEKATALOG XI, 1916/17 und AUFNAHMEKATALOG XXXIII, 1919/20).

1923/24

Ilse Wallentin, born on April 26, 1895 in Vienna was the first female doctoral student at the BOKU Vienna. Her dissertation title was: 'Trials with different planting distances of Coriandrum sativum, Pimpinella anisum and Digitalis lanata' (RIGOROSENAKTEN, 1906–1940).

1936

Helvig Schütte, married to Mr. Habsburg-Lothringen, is the first alumna in forestry. She refuted former statements of male professors and rectors claiming that women studying are unfeminine and – for biological reasons – less suitable for studies. Women had to prove their qualification for studies through accomplishing an internship (JOHANN, 2010, 30f).

1939–1945

Second World War

1945

Foundation of the study programme of brewing and fermentation technology/zymotechnology. About 60 % of the students were women since it was associated with 'the feminine' and not yet gender-specifically classified (MAURER, 1987, 116).

1949

'One is not born a woman, one becomes a woman.' In her book 'The Second Sex', Simone de Beauvoir examines the consequences of gender difference (BEAUVOIR, 2015).

1957

On the initiative of the Austrian Trade Union Federation, a maternity leave with a duration of 6 months – at this time, however, still unpaid – was introduced. The Maternity Protection Act dating back to the NS era was substituted (SPÖ, 2011).

1960

Maternity leave in Austria becomes paid leave and is extended to one year (ibid., 2011).

1965/66

7.5 % of the students at the BOKU Vienna are women. Out of 9,403 female students, at all Austrian universities, 107 (1.1 %) study at the BOKU Vienna.

1979

Bruno Kreisky, Federal Chancellor of Austria (1970–1983), separates the field of women's policy from the field of family policy. With Johanna Dohnal as State Secretary for Women's Issues, women's policy in Austria becomes institutionalised. In her position, she enables the implementation of political measures relevant for women, as for example the extension of maternity protection to female farmers and (commercially) self-employed women (SPÖ, 2011).

1981

Ingeborg Dirmhirn became the first female professor at the BOKU Vienna. She had already held this position (in the USA) since 1968 (BOKU, 2008). The study programme 'Landscape Ecology and Landscape Gardening' was introduced. In the winter term of 1985/86, 21.3 % of the 1,167 women studying at the BOKU Vienna chose this branch of study (MAURER, 1987, 120).

Anjoulie Brandner, Aurélie Karlinger

1985

The term 'gender mainstreaming'[1] is first introduced at the 3rd UN Women's Conference in Nairobi (UN Women, 2016). The Austrian Students' Union at the BOKU Vienna (ÖH BOKU) installs a Women's Department for administrative affairs (BOKU, 1985, 92).

1985/86

1,167 (4.7 %), out of 24,732 women at all Austrian universities, are enrolled at the BOKU Vienna (MAURER, 1987, 116ff).

1990

It comes to an 'explosion' of discourses on the gender category – initially in English-speaking countries, from 1933 onwards, however, also in the German-speaking world – leading to large controversies on the concept of gender. The differentiation between 'sex' and 'gender'[2] is introduced to the feminist discourse by the second women's movement in the United States and Great Britain (FREY, 2003).

1992

Foundation of the European Union by the EC member states on the basis of the Maastricht Treaty (EU, 2016).

1993

'One has to consciously adopt the female role.' With 'An Ethics of Sexual Difference', Luce Irigaray primarily refers to main schools of thought on gender difference (IRIGARAY, 1985 und 1991).

Equal opportunities[3] are included as a goal into the structural funds of the European Union. Gender mainstreaming is understood as a cross-sectional matter and aims at being integrated into the entire social and economic policies.

1996

Gender mainstreaming becomes a main focus in the 4th Action Programme of the European Union (1996–2000). The European Union commits itself to the implementation of gender mainstreaming as a central strategy in the equality policy in the Communication 'Incorporating equal opportunities for women and men into all Community policies and activities' (BAER, 2012).

1997

The Treaty of Amsterdam sets the legal framework for the gender mainstreaming strategy on the European level (coming into force only 2 years later) (EU, 2016).

1998

Since 1998, the principle of equality of the Federal Constitutional Law has set a legal framework for the gender mainstreaming strategy on the Austrian level (B-VG, 2016).

```
──────────────2000──────────────────2020────────────────────────────▶
```

2000

Between 2000 and 2006, the equality policy is to be incorporated into all structural funds (ERDF, ESF, EAGGF and FIFG) of the European Union and structural programmes financed by those funds (EU, 2001).

2007–2009

Ingela Bruner becomes the first female rector at the BOKU Vienna and throughout Austria (BOKU, 2014).

2010–2015

EU's strategy for equality between women and men; five-year strategy of the European Commission for more equal opportunities for women and men in Europe. Measures to promote equal opportunities focus on economy and labour market, equal pay for equal work, equality in decision-making positions, combating gender-based violence and enhancing gender equality outside the European Union (EU, 2010).

2013

At the BOKU Vienna:
Regular students: 48 % women, 52 % men. Academic degrees: 52 % women, 48 % men. University professors: 14 women, 51 men. (For comparison: At the TU Vienna, 14 out of 137 professorships are held by women.)
Female university professors (§ 98 UG) at the BOKU Vienna earn 6.6 % less than their male colleagues. Female assistant professors earn even 10.2 % less in comparison to their male colleagues (BMWFW, 2013).

2013

At all Austrian universities:
Regular students: 53 % women, 47 % men. Academic degrees: 59 % women, 41 % men. At Austrian universities, 494 professorships out of a total of 2,265 professorships are held by women (BMWFW, 2013).

2014–2020

New funding period:
Also for this programme period a dual approach to gender equality is to be applied which is characterised by the combination of gender mainstreaming with specific measures (ESF, 2014).

2015/16

Students according to branch of study at the BOKU Vienna (Bachelor and Master programmes, refer to BOKU, 2015):
Forestry/Forest Sciences: 384 women, 968 men.
Civil Engineering and Water Management:
495 women, 1123 men.
Landscape Planning and Landscape Architecture:
916 women, 580 men.
Agricultural Sciences: 1272 women, 1229 men.
Food Science and Biotechnology: 278 women, 164 men.
Environment and Bio-Resources Management:
1407 women, 1215 men.

[1] Gender mainstreaming

Gender mainstreaming is considered to be a strategy of equality policy and was given a legal framework in the EU's primary law by the Treaty of Amsterdam in 1997/99. It obliges the member states of the European Union to an active equality policy. The strategy of gender mainstreaming is an explicit commitment to the enhancement of the objective of gender equality through a focus on reducing inequalities in all political and planning fields (DAMYANOVIC, 2007, 25).

[2] 'Sex' and 'gender'

The differentiation between 'sex' and 'gender' was introduced to the feminist discourse by the second women's movement in Great Britain and the USA. The initially in the English-speaking countries merely grammatically introduced term 'gender' was modified to a social-theoretical one by the British sociologist Ann Oakley. Ann Oakley distinguishes the terms 'gender' and 'sex' from each other by referring to 'sex' as characterising the biological differences between women and men and to 'gender' as something socially constructed. Since this differentiation does not exist in the German-speaking countries, the terms 'sex' and 'gender' were adopted (FREY, 2003, 75ff).

[3] Equal opportunity

'Equal opportunity means that women and men have the same chances to participate in the economic, political, social and cultural life by their own free decision. [...] Equal opportunity as the goal of gender mainstreaming means that all policies and measures have to be shaped in a way that they do not produce inequalities but enhance equal opportunities' (PIMMINGER, 2001, 16ff).

[4] Treaty of Amsterdam (1997/99)

'The implementation of gender mainstreaming in the political guidelines, laws, directives and funding programmes throughout Europe has its legal basis in the European primary law. The Treaty of Amsterdam (1997/99) obliges the member states of the European Union to an active equality policy in terms of gender ' (DAMYANOVIC, 2007, 25).

[5] Principle of equality

The principle of equality states that 'All Federal nationals are equal before the law. Privileges based upon birth, sex, estate, class or religion are excluded' (Article 7 paragraph 1, Federal Constitutional Law). Paragraph 2 of Article 7 stipulates that 'The Federation, Laender and municipalities subscribe to the de-facto equality of men and women. Measures to promote factual equality of women and men, particularly by eliminating actually existing inequalities, are admissible' (B-VG, 2016).

[6] Gender equality

'Gender equality means that both sexes are equally present, competent and involved in all fields of public life. [...] Objective is the promotion of the involvement of women and men in all social spheres; gender equality must be ensured and supported' (BMSG, 1999, 3).

REFERENCES

BAER, Susanne (2012): Geschichte von GM international und EU, Gender Kompetenz Zentrum, Humboldt-Universität zu Berlin, http://www.genderkompetenz.info/genderkompetenz-2003–2010/gender-mainstreaming/Grundlagen/geschichten/international/index.html/ (access on 08.07.2016)

BEAUVOIR, Simone de. (2015): Das (zweite) andere Geschlecht – der Dirskurs „Frau" im Wandel, Frank und Timme GmbH Verlag für wissenschaftliche Literatur, Berlin.

BMSG – Bundesministerium für Soziale Sicherheit und Generationen, Sektion für Frauenangelegenheiten (Hg.) (1999): Gender Mainstreaming. Begriffsschema, Methodologie und Darstellung nachahmenswerter Praktiken. Abschließender Bericht der Mainstreaming Expertengruppe (EG-S-MC) des Europarates.

BMWFW – Bundesministerium für Wissenschaft, Forschung und Wirtschaft: Datawarehouse Hochschulbereich: https://oravm13.noc-science.at/apex/f?p=103:36:0::NO::: (access on 08.07.2016)

BOKU – Universität für Bodenkultur Wien (1985): Vorlesungsverzeichnis 1984/85.

BOKU – Universität für Bodenkultur Wien (2014): Über die BOKU: Geschichte: RektorInnen. https://www.boku.ac.at/universitaetsleitung/rektorat/stabsstellen/oeffentlichkeitsarbeit/themen/geschichte/rektorinnen/ (access on 08.07.2016)

BOKU – Universität für Bodenkultur Wien (2015): Studierendenstatistik.

BOKU – Universität für Bodenkultur Wien (2008): Tod von Prof. Dirmhirn. https://www.boku.ac.at/news/newsitem/2664/ (access on 08.07.2016)

B-VG – Bundes-Verfassungsgesetz (2016): Artikel 7 Abs. 1, BGBl. Nr. 1/1930 idF BGBl. I Nr. 41/2016, Fassung 08.09.2016, https://www.ris.bka.gv.at/GeltendeFassung.wxe?Abfrage=Bundesnormen&Gesetzesnummer=10000138 (access on 08.07.2016)

DAMYANOVIC, Doris (2007): Landschaftsplanung als Qualitätssicherung zur Umsetzung der Strategie des Gender Mainstreaming. Guthmann-Peterson, Wien.

DEUTSCHER BUNDESTAG (2016): Einführungsdaten des Frauenwahlrechts in 20 europäischen Ländern, https://www.bundestag.de/kulturundgeschichte/ausstellungen/parl_hist/frauenwahlrecht/einfuehrung/246998 (access on 08.07.2016)

EFS – AGENTUR FÜR GLEICHSTELLUNG IM ESF (2014) Vorbereitungen der Strukturfondsförderperiode 2014–2020, http://www.esf-gleichstellung.de/142.html (access on 08.07.2016)

EU – Europäische Union (2016): EU-Verträge, http://europa.eu/eu-law/decision-making/treaties/index_de.htm (access on08.07.2016)

EU – Europäische Union (2001): Bericht der Kommission – 13. Jahresbericht der Strukturfonds, http://eur-lex.europa.eu/legal-content/DE/TXT/?uri=celex%3A52002DC0591 (access on 08.07.2016)

EU – Europäische Union (2010): Mitteilung der Kommission an das europäische Parlament, den Rat, den europäischen wirtschafts- und Sozialausschuss und den Ausschuss der Regionen Strategie für die Gleichstellung von Frauen und Männern 2010–2015, Brüssel, http://eur-lex.europa.eu/legal-content/DE/ALL/?uri=CELEX:52010DC0491 (access on 08.07.2016)

FREY, Regina (2003): Gender im Mainstreaming – Geschlechtertheorie und -praxis im internationalen Diskurs. Ulrike Helmer Verlag, Königstein/Taunus.

IRIGARAY, Luce (1985): This Sex Which is Not One, Ithaca (dt. 1979, S.76f). In: FACH, Wolfgang (1994): Not der Tugend – Tugend der Not: Frauenalltag und feministische Theorie, Leske und Budrich, Obladen.

IRIGARAY Luce (1991): Ethik der sexuellen Differenz, Suhrkamp, Frankfurt am Main.

PIMMINGER, Irene (2001): Handbuch Gender Mainstreaming in der Regionalentwicklung – Einführung in die Programmplanung, Bundesministerium für Bildung, Wissenschaft und Kultur (Hg.), Forschungsprogramm Kulturlandschaft, Wien, 2001.

SPÖ – Bundesgeschäftsstelle, Sozialdemokratische Partei Österreichs Bundesorganisation (2016): Für Österreich – Meilensteine der Ära Kreisky, Wien, http://www.kreisky100.at/meilensteine/index.html (access on 08.07.2016) UN WOMEN – Nationalkomitee Österreich (2016): UN-Weltfrauenkonferenzen, http://www.unwomen-nc.at/ueber-uns/begriffserklaerungen/ (access on 08.07.2016)

LITERATURE PROVIDED BY PETER WILTSCHE FROM THE UNIVERSITY ARCHIVE OF THE BOKU VIENNA

AUFNAHMEKATALOG XI für außerordentliche Hörer der Hochschule für Bodenkultur, Eintrag 242 und AUFNAHMEKATALOG XXXIII für ordentliche Hörer der Hochschule für Bodenkultur, Eintrag 300, Studienabschluss mit III. Landwirtschaftlicher Staatsprüfung am 14. Juli 1922.

BAUER, Josef (1927): Das Frauenstudium an der Hochschule für Bodenkultur. In: Dreißig Jahre Frauenstudium in Österreich 1987 bis 1927. Festausschuss anlässlich des dreißigjährigen Frauenstudiumjubiläums (Hg.) Wien.

GRASSLER, Monika (o.J.): Frauenstudium. In: Zeitung zwischen Universität, Städtele und Land, zwischen StudentInnen und ÖH. Hochschülerschaft an der Universität für Bodenkultur, Wien (Hg.).

JOHANN, Elisabeth (2010): 90 Jahre „grünes" Frauenstudium. In: Forstzeitung. Österreichischer Agrarverlag.

MAURER, Margarete (1987): Frauen an der Hochschule für Bodenkultur: Studium und Berufsmöglichkeiten. In: Verband der Akademikerinnen Österreichs (Hg.): Frauenstudium und akademische Frauenarbeit in Österreich. Wien, S. 115–130.

PRIMOST, Edith (1968): Der Weg zur Gleichberechtigung innerhalb der Rechtsordnung: Ein historischer Überblick. Nicht veröffentlicht.

RIGOROSENAKTEN der Hochschule für Bodenkultur 1906–1940, Rigorosum am 15. Mai 1924.

PORTRÄTS

PORTRAITS

Frauenporträts
Women's portraits

Ulrike Böker
trained kindergarten teacher, politics
Christine Itzlinger
spatial planner, administration
Martina Jauschneg
landscape planner, planning office
Eva Kail
spatial planner, administration
Jutta Kleedorfer
spatial planner, administration
Bente Knoll
landscape planner, planning office
Theresia Oedl-Wieser .
agricultural economist, administration
Hanna Posch
landscape planner, planing office
Gerda Schneider
landscape planner, university
Susanne Staller
landscape planner, planing office
Heide Studer
landscape planner, planing office
Sibylla Zech
spatial planner, university, planning office
Helga Lassy
architect, architectural practice
Margarete Schütte-Lihotzky
architect, architectural practice

Mitwirkende StudentInnen
Participating students

BOKU Wien BOKU Vienna

Anjoulie Brandner
Sabine Luger
Elena Reischauer
Aurélie Karlinger
Carina Diesenreiter
Andrea Dobersberger
Johanna Jani
Heidrun Wankiewicz
Anna Grube

TU Wien TU Vienna

Marie-Sophie Plakolm
Anca Dumitrescu
Evelyn Lavinia Bojic
Christine Wallmüller
Alexander Schraml
Dajana Saric
Raluca Maria Pintescu-Schipor
Bianca-Ana Moldovan

On Stage! Vienna, Stop 2014
Coordinators: Doris Damyanovic, Petra Hirschler, Gesa Witthöft
Guest lecture: Eva Álvarez
Co-supervision: Karin Weber, Hannah Jenal
Financial support: Office for Gender Competence,
University of Technology Vienna; Office for Feminist Politics,
Austrian Students' Union, BOKU Vienna; Department of Landscape,
Spatial and Infrastructure Sciences; Equal Opportunities Working
Partys Office; Coordination Center for Equal Opportunities,
Advancement of Women and Gender Studies; University Library
and University Archive (UB), all BOKU Vienna

Ulrike Böker

„*Das Tun an sich ist schon wirklich etwas Wirkungsvolles.*"

'*Merely taking action is already effective by itself.*'

Ulrike Böker war schon immer davon überzeugt, dass Unterschiede zwischen Mann und Frau vorhanden sind, dass Frauen jedoch denselben Stellenwert und dieselbe Gestaltungskraft haben wie Männer. Es ist ihr bewusst, dass mehr Frauen in die machtvollen Positionen gelangen müssen. Wie schon als Bürgermeisterin, so auch jetzt als Abgeordnete zum Oberösterreichischen (Oö.) Landtag, nützt Ulrike Böker ihre Position gerne, um diese Belange zu thematisieren, und sagt: „Macht kann man missbrauchen oder gestalterisch damit umgehen."

Sie selbst war im Laufe ihres Lebens insbesondere in den Bereichen Kunst und Kultur tätig und immer wieder Teil sowie Mitbegründerin diverser Gruppen, die sich mit dem Thema Gleichstellung und Chancengleichheit befassen, wie zum Beispiel der ‚Vernetzungsstelle für Frauen in Kunst und Kultur (FIFTITU%)' und des Netzwerks „Weibs- und Mannsbilder der Region Urfahr West (uwe) für gendergerechte Lebensräume". Als Mitinitiatorin eines einmal im Jahr stattfindenden, österreichweiten Bürgermeisterinnentreffens unterstützt sie Initiativen, die Frauen auf die Bühne bringen. Das soll wiederum andere dazu anstiften, sich auch zuzutrauen, nach vorne zu treten.

Ihrer Ansicht nach unbedingt notwendig sind Veränderungen und Strukturen, die ein Arbeitsmodell erlauben, in dem Frauen und Männer gleichberechtigt an den monetären wie nichtmonetären Aufgaben teilnehmen.

In ihrer Rolle als Bauherrin, welche sie als Bürgermeisterin inne hatte, sieht sie auf jeden Fall im öffentlichen Raum und in der Raumordnung Handlungsbedarf und Veränderungspotenzial. Obwohl sie selbst keine Planerin ist, sieht sie die Notwendigkeit für mögliche Treffpunkte im öffentlichen Raum, um ohne Konsumzwang dort etwas tun zu können und die Möglichkeit zu schaffen, Gemeinsamkeiten zu leben.

Ulrike Böker has always had the self-concept that although there are biological differences between men and women, she – being a woman – definitely has the same status and creative power as men. She is aware of the fact that there is a lot to do about the issue of women in powerful positions. As former mayoress as well as member of the provincial parliament of Upper Austria today, Ulrike Böker benefits willingly from her position to make these issues subject of discussion.

Personally, she has always been part of initiatives working and dealing with art and culture and been a co-initiator of diverse groups considering principles of equalisation and equal opportunities as for example the 'Vernetzungsstelle für Frauen in Kunst und Kultur (FIFTITU%)' and the network 'Weibs- und Mannsbilder der Region Urfahr West (uwe) für gendergerechte Lebensräume'. Moreover, as a co-initiator of an Austria-wide annual mayoresses meeting, she supports initiatives where 'the stage' is given to the women. The target is to incite other women to join and take confidence in themselves, to step out from the back and move into the foreground.

In Ulrike Böker's opinion, structural changes are absolutely necessary in order to create a working scheme which allows men and women to equally take part in monetary as well as non-monetary tasks, which, however, implies men's retreat from powerful positions.

In her role as developer, which she held during her time being mayoress, she definitely sees need for action and potential for change in public space as well as in the field of spatial planning. Although she is not a planner, she perceives the necessity of creating possibilities to meet in public space without pressure to consume, in order to 'live' commonalities.

1956
geboren in Linz als 2. Tochter des Schneidermeisters Alois und der mithelfenden Hausfrau Rosina Simader. Kindergarten; viel Freiraum als Kind erlebt, da beide Elternteile sehr beschäftigt waren – viel bei der Donau und beim „Wäscheplatzl" (öffentlicher Raum) gespielt

1974
Arbeit in einer Akkord-Schneiderei – nicht lange ausgehalten!

1975–2000
ständiger Wechsel zwischen monetären und nichtmonetären Arbeiten (Haushalt, Job, Kindererziehung, Ehrenamt, etc.)

1991
Geburt des 2. Sohnes Paul; 2,5 Jahre zu Hause beim Sohn; Scheidung

1997
6 Jahre Vorstandtätigkeit KUPF (Kulturplattform Oö.) und Verein FIFTITU%; Mitbegründerin einer BürgerInnenliste in Ottensheim; Büroleiterin „Festival der Regionen"; dazwischen im Kulturwirtshaus ihrer Schwester gearbeitet; Organisationsassistenz „Meisterklasse Architektur" Kunstuni Linz

1960
VS Ottensheim; HS Ottensheim; 4-jährige Fachschule für Damen- und Herrenkleider

1975
Geburt der 1. Tochter Ute; Ausbildung zur Kindergärtnerin

1979
Geburt der 2. Tochter Johanna

1980
Arbeit als Kindergartenpädagogin; intensive ehrenamtliche Mitarbeit in der Kulturgruppe „arge granit"; Geburt des 3. Kindes (Sohn Florian); teilzeitbeschäftigt im Architekturbüro ihres damaligen Mannes; altes Haus in Ottensheim an der Donau gekauft und mühsam und lange um- und neugebaut

2000
Geschäftsführerin „Festival der Regionen", Projektleiterin des Stationentheaters „Barbaren"; Gemeinderätin ab 1998; 2003 Bürgermeisterin; 2009 zum 2. Mal als Bürgermeisterin gewählt

2015
Abgeordnete zum Oö. Landtag

von li. o. nach re. u. © Ulrike Böker, o. J.; Gemeindeamt Ottensheim, 2012

113

Engagement als Bürgermeisterin & Projekte in der Gemeinde

Commitment as Mayoress & Projects in the Municipality

Ort
Gemeinde Ottensheim, Oberösterreich

Realisierte Projekte im Zeitrahmen 2010–2013
Wochenmarkt (seit 1996)
OTELO Offenes Technologielabor (2011)
Neue Mittelschule Ottensheim (2012)
Neues Gemeindeamt (2010)
Begegnungszone Shared Space Linzerstraße (2013)

Location
Municipality of Ottensheim, Upper Austria

Projects realised during 2010–2013
Weekly market (since 1996)
OTELO open technology lab (2011)
New secondary school (2012)
New municipal office building (2010)
Shared space Linzerstraße (2013)

Wochenmarkt
Seit über 20 Jahren, wöchentlich stattfindender Markt, regionale, saisonale Produkte.
Weekly market
For over 20 years; farmer's market, regional and seasonal products.

© Aurélie Karlinger, 2013

OTELO Offenes Technologielabor
Teilweise Nutzung des leerstehenden alten Amtshauses; Raum für vielseitige Ideen, kreative, technische Aktivitäten, Bildung, Forschung, Wissenschaft, Politik und Medien; gemeinsames Entwickeln von Projekten und Ideen, Beiträge zum Gemeinwohl.
OTELO open technology lab
partial use of the vacant former municipal office building; space for creative and technical activities; research, education, science, politics and media; collective elaboration of projects and ideas as contribution to public welfare.

© Ulrike Böker, 2012

© Aurélie Karlinger, 2013

Neue Mittelschule Ottensheim

Sanierung der Gebäude sowie Neugestaltung des Innenhofs; Bau einer neuen Bibliothek. Ausstattung mit schräger Liegewiese, multifunktionalem Ballspielplatz, Grünfläche mit Sitzstufen; barrierefreier Zugang.
Planung: Architekt Adalbert Böker

New secondary school
refurbishment of school buildings, redesign of schoolyard and construction of a school library; equipped with a sloping relaxing lawn, multifunctional ball games area, green area with seating steps; barrier-free access.
Design: Adalbert Böker, architect

© SUE Architekten, 2010; Ulrike Böker, 2012

Neues Gemeindeamt

Entwicklung im Ortskern; Leerstandsthematik; Verwandlung eines verwahrlosten Bauwerks in ein offenes und einladendes Gemeindezentrum.
Planung: SUE Architekten_Wien

New municipal office building
Vacancy problem and revival of town centre; transformation of the abandoned and neglected building into an open and friendly municipal centre.
Design: SUE Architekten_Wien

© Shared Space Fotoclub Ottensheim, o. J.

Begegnungszone „Shared Space" Linzerstraße

Marktplatz – mittlerweile gesamter Ortskern
2011 wurden zwei Straßenabschnitte nach dem „Shared Space" Prinzip gestaltet. Der Ortskern ist seit Dezember 2013 Begegnungszone.

Shared space Linzerstraße
In 2011, two street sections were designed according to the principles of shared space; whole town centre is shared space zone since 2013.

DI^{in} Christine Itzlinger

„Planen ist mehr, als das eigene Weltbild fortzuschreiben."

'Planning is more than constantly updating one's own worldview.'

Von klein auf wollte Christine Itzlinger beweisen, dass Mädchen gleich gut und gleich viel wert sind wie Buben. Denn als eines von drei Mädchen in einem Dorf geboren, erlebte sie, wie „gute Freunde" ihrem Vater nach der Geburt der Schwester Büchsen vor die Haustüre stellten – ein Spott-Zeichen für einen Mann, der nur Töchter hatte. Augenöffner waren für Christine Itzlinger Bücher wie „Die Töchter Egalias" von Gerd Brantenberg oder „Die Scham ist vorbei" von Anja Meulenbelt. Während des Raumplanungsstudiums an der TU Wien übernahm sie die „patriarchalen Planungszugänge und den männlichen Blick auf die (Planungs-) Welt". Gender-Fragen, Frauenplanung oder Diversität waren für sie während der Ausbildung noch keine Themen.

Ihre Berufslaufbahn begann als Sachbearbeiterin in der örtlichen Raumplanung des Landes Salzburg, zu der sie 2007 als Leiterin zurückkehrte. Währenddessen wechselte sie in die überörtliche Raumplanung, wo sie maßgeblich an der ambitionierten Raumordnungsgesetz-Novelle 2009 und an der Erstellung des Raumordnungssachprogrammes „Siedlungsentwicklung und Betriebsstandorte im Salzburger Zentralraum" beteiligt war. Planungsprinzipien wie „Stadt/Region der kurzen Wege" oder „am Öffentlichen Verkehr orientierte Siedlungsentwicklung für Wohnen und Gewerbe" waren einige der planerischen Eckpunkte für eine „alltagsgerechte Region Salzburg und Umland". Als sie 2002 als Referentin der Tagung „Wir planen für Männer und Frauen" eingeladen wurde, war dies ein Anknüpfen an inzwischen verschüttetes Wissen und Denken.

Mit GenderAlp! systematisierte sie die Suche nach dem „Was ist anders, wenn man Gender Mainstreaming in die Planung integriert?". Dieses von ihr mitgetragene Projekt legte den Grundstein für Methoden, Begriffe und weitergehende Diskussionen über die Frage, wie Gender in die Planung kommt und diese verändert. 2007 übernahm sie die Leitung des Referats Örtliche Raumplanung im Land Salzburg. Der geschlechtssensible Blick, wenn erst einmal geweckt, geht nicht mehr verloren. Darum die Warnung: Gender Planning kann Ihre Weltsicht verändern!

Since her childhood Christine Itzlinger has wanted to prove that girls are on par with boys. As one of three sisters, she had to see how her father was exposed to public ridicule as he had 'only' daughters. Later, gender equality became an issue to her through reading feminist books. 'Egalia's Daughters' by the Norwegian writer Gerd Brantenberg or 'The Shame is Over' by Anja Meulenbelt opened a door to a new world for her. Christine Itzlinger's choice of studies was a technical field: she graduated in spatial planning at the TU Vienna, where she learned how to plan with patriarchal planning norms and male views on planning. Neither gender issues nor women's topics or diversity were then part of the lectures.

She initiated her working career at the regional planning department of the Provincial Government of Salzburg and became its head in 2007. Meanwhile she worked on the spatial strategy for settlement and industrial sites in Greater Salzburg and took part in the amendment of the spatial planning law in 2009. When she was invited as speaker at a conference on planning for women and men in 2002, she felt like rediscovering lost thinking and knowledge. Since then, Christine Itzlinger has been researching on the topic and integrating gender planning and gender mainstreaming into her work: starting with her active involvement in the GenderAlp! project, she is still passionate to improve living qualities for women and men by implementing planning principles such as city/region of short distances, public transport for dwellers and workers as well as requirement-oriented planning for everyday life in Salzburg. In January 2007, she became director of the local planning department of the Provincial Government of Salzburg. She keeps on 'being gender sensitive in all her activities without explicitly using the still irritating term gender.' Attention: Gender Planning can change your worldview!

1967
Geburt

1973
Das 3-Mäderlhaus ist komplett. Vater wird als „Büchsenmacher" tituliert

1980/83
Die Zeit der Lektüre: „Die Töchter Egalias" von Gerd Brantenberg und „Häutungen" von Verena Stefan etc.

1986
Beginn Studium Raumplanung

2002
Referentin, Tagung: „Wir planen für Männer und Frauen"

2004–2007
GenderAlp!

2007
Leiterin des Referats „Örtliche Raumplanung" in Salzburg

GenderAlp! – Raumentwicklung für Frauen und Männer

GenderAlp! – Spatial Development for Women and Men

Bearbeitungszeitraum Project Period
2005–2007

Ort Location
Salzburg

AuftraggeberInnen Principal Investigators
Land Salzburg / EU-Alpenraumprogramm
Provincial Government of Salzburg / Alpine Space Programme

ProjektpartnerInnen Project Partners
AT: Niederösterreich, Oberösterreich
Institut für Landschaftsplanung, BOKU Wien
IT: Provinz Genua, Regional-Agentur LAMORO
FR: Region Rhone-Alpen
SI: Institut für Stadtplanung, Republik Slowenien
D: Stadt München, Stadt Freiburg/Breisgau
AT: Lower Austria, Upper Austria, Institute of Landscape
Planning, BOKU Vienna
IT: Province of Genoa, Regional Agency LAMORO
FR: Region of Rhône-Alpes
SI: Urban Planning Institute of the Republic of Slovenia
GER: City of Munich, City of Freiburg/Breisgau

Projektmanagement Project management
planwind.at, Salzburg

GenderAlp! wurde vom Büro für Frauenfragen und Chancengleichheit des Landes Salzburg initiiert, um praktische Erfahrungen und Methoden für die Umsetzung von Gender Mainstreaming in der Raumplanung, in der Regionalentwicklung und in der Förderung weiter zu entwickeln. Im Rahmen von GenderAlp!, das von 01/2005–12/2007 als „ProjektHolding" organisiert war, wurden 33 Praxisprojekte der PartnerInnen in ihren Städten und Regionen umgesetzt.

Eines der Salzburger Praxisprojekte war die Anwendung der Gender Mainstreaming Strategie auf den Prozess und die Planungsinhalte des neuen Raumordnungssachprogrammes „Siedlungsentwicklung und Betriebsstandorte im Salzburger Zentralraum". Bereits 2004 wurde eine geschlechterdifferenzierte Regionalanalyse erstellt. Eine Sammlung von Gender Planning Umsetzungsbeispielen aus Deutschland und der Schweiz zeigte auf, welche Festlegungen in der Planung sinnvoll und wirkungsvoll sind. Darauf bauten die neuen Ziele und Maßnahmen auf, die in der Folge auf ihre Wirkungen auf Frauen und Männer geprüft wurden. Prinzipien wie die Stadtregion der kurzen Wege, soziale Infrastruktur und ÖV-Anschluss als Muss für Siedlungserweiterung und Nutzungsmischung waren wichtige inhaltliche Schwerpunkte.

Das neue Sachprogramm wurde 2009 unter dem Titel „Wohnen und Arbeiten im Salzburger Zentralraum" für die Planungen wirksam.

The project 'GenderAlp!' was initiated by the Office for Equal Opportunities and Women's Affairs of the Provincial Government Salzburg with the main goal to collect and develop practical tools on how to implement gender mainstreaming in spatial planning, in regional development and in financial support.

GenderAlp! has developed its partnership of experienced partners, its working programme and its budget as a teamwork of 4 partners: namely the Office for Equal Opportunities and Women's Affairs, the Department of Spatial Planning (both Provincial Government of Salzburg) and the consultants Elke Portugall (Munich) and Heidrun Wankiewicz (Salzburg).

GenderAlp! has been implemented as a project holding where 33 practice projects had been done in all partner cities and regions.

One of the Salzburg practice projects on gender planning has been a revision of the spatial strategy on settlement development and operating sites in the Greater Salzburg region. The project started with a gender-differentiated regional analysis which was followed by a good practice collection of gender planning tools from Germany and Switzerland. An assessment of the new targets and measures as regards gender impact and a strong role of gender issues in decision making was taken into consideration.

The new spatial strategy was implemented in March 2009.

© Land Salzburg, Raumplanung, 2009

© Land Salzburg/GenderAlp!, 2007

© planwind.at, 2012

© Land Salzburg/GenderAlp!, 2007

DIⁱⁿ Martina Jauschneg

„Gender macht Vielfalt sichtbar."
'Gender makes diversity visible.'

Martina Jauschneg setzte sich als junge Studentin im Rahmen verschiedener Lehrveranstaltungen mit frauenspezifischen Themen in Bezug auf räumliche Planung auseinander. So erlebte sie ihren Einstieg in feministische Denkweisen, den sie im Kreise selbst organisierter Frauen-Lese-Diskussions-Gruppen vertiefte. Neben der Reflexion der eigenen Situation und des gegenseitigen Empowerments standen die Analyse von geschlechterspezifischen gesellschaftlichen Ungleichheiten und vor allem die Möglichkeiten, diese zu beheben, im Mittelpunkt. Heute hebt Martina Jauschneg als wichtigen Teil ihres beruflichen Erfolges ihr aus dieser Zeit stammendes Netzwerk aus Kolleginnen hervor, das sie unter anderem darin bestärkt, beruflich ihr eigenes „Ding" zu machen.

Als besonders bedeutsame Mentorin erwies sich Inge Meta Hülbusch, Landschaftsplanerin einer etwas älteren Generation aus Deutschland, die die Lehrveranstaltung „Frauen in der Geschichte der Landschaftsplanung und Gartenkunst" an der BOKU Wien abhielt und im Zuge dieser auch von sich erzählte. Auf Martina Jauschneg wirkten diese Erzählungen aus Inge Metas Leben und ihre Erfahrungen als Frau, Mutter und Planerin sehr interessant und auch ermutigend – insbesondere bei ihrem Einstieg ins Berufsleben.

Martina Jauschnegs Zugang zum Thema Gender Mainstreaming hat sich im Laufe der Jahre geändert, und der anfänglich stark analytische, „verstehen-wollende" Zugang hat sich in einer reflexiven Lebensgrundhaltung gewandelt, da die Kategorie „Geschlecht" immer eine Rolle spielt. Gender Mainstreaming bedeutet für sie, vermeintliche gesellschaftliche Normen in Frage zu stellen, durch Interventionen mehr Chancengleichheit für alle zu erreichen und die Vielfalt der Lebensentwürfe und der Geschlechter sichtbarer zu machen.

Martina Jauschnegs Lebensgestaltung ist vielseitig: Sie ist Mutter von Zwillingssöhnen, teilt sich die Erziehung der Kinder mit dem Vater nach dem Modell der „Doppelresidenz", ist als Lektorin an der BOKU Wien tätig und führt ein Büro für Landschaftsplanung.

As a student, Martina Jauschneg dealt with feminist issues connected to planning in the framework of various lectures. Hence, she experienced her own approach towards the feminist way of thinking, which she deepened among self-organised women reading circles. Besides the reflection of her own position and the mutual empowerments, the analysis of gender specific, societal inequalities and especially the possibilities to eliminate those, stood in the focus. Today, Martina Jauschneg highlights her professional success as linked to her network of colleagues originating from this period and which encouraged her to do 'her own (professional) thing'.

Especially important to her, was Inge Meta Hülbusch, a German landscape planner of an earlier generation. At university, Hülbusch led a course named 'Women in the history of landscape planning and garden art' at the BOKU Vienna, in which she also talked about herself and her experiences as a woman, mother and planner. For Martina Jauschneg, those stories were very interesting and encouraging – especially for initiating her own working life.

Martina Jauschneg's personal approach towards gender mainstreaming has changed over time and her former analytical approach has become manifest in her attitude towards life. Gender mainstreaming to her, means to question apparent societal norms and to uncover the versatile aspects of life plans.

Martina Jauschneg's own life plan reflects this manifoldness: She is a mother of twin boys, shares the responsibilities of child rearing with their father on the basis of a 'double residence', is lecturer at BOKU Vienna and holds an own planning office.

1975
Geburt

1980
Kindergarten Großklein

1981
Volksschule Großklein

1985
AHS Leibnitz

1990
fächerübergreifende Matura Biologie/Philosophie: „Unterschied Sex & Gender"

1994
Beginn Studium „Landschaftsplanung und Landschaftspflege"

1996
Arbeitskreis für Frauen in Naturwissenschaft und Technik; Frauen in Planung und Architektur; die.plan.werkerinnen

2001
Abschluss des Studiums, Diplomarbeit: „I moch d'Orbeit zu 99 % allan!" – Handlungsfreiräume und Perspektiven in den Lebensplänen der Bäuerinnen – ein landschaftsplanerischer Beitrag zur Landbewirtschaftung am Beispiel von zwölf Hofwirtschaften im Naturpark Südsteirisches Weinland

2002
Geburt der beiden Söhne

2004–2005
Gartengestalterin

2005–2008
Wissenschaftliche Mitarbeiterin

ab 2008
Lektorin an der BOKU Wien (Übungen mit Feldarbeiten zur Landschaftsplanung, Frauen in der Geschichte der Landschaftsplanung und Gartenkunst)

2009
Gründung des Ingenieurinnen-Büros

2011
Gründung des Forschungsvereins „Green City Lab"

ECOMOB –
Equal Chances of Mobility in Rural Space
Planerischer Beitrag zur Gewährleistung einer sicheren und sozialverträglichen Mobilität von Jugendlichen im ländlichen Raum

ECOMOB –
Equal Chances of Mobility in Rural Space
Planning Contribution to Ensure a Safe and Socially Acceptable Mobility for Adolescents in Rural Areas

Bearbeitungszeitraum Project Period
Jänner–Dezember 2009 January–December 2009

Ort Location
Straden, Steiermark Styria

Fördergeber Funding sponsor
Programmlinie IV2Splus/ways2go des Bundesministeriums für Verkehr, Innovation und Technologie
Programme Line IV2Splus/ways2go of the Federal Ministry for Transport, Innovation and Technology

Einordnung Key Words
Motivforschung zur Ableitung des gruppenspezifischen Mobilitätsbedarfs und der Ansprüche von Jugendlichen im ländlichen Raum an die Verkehrssysteme der Zukunft
Research in the context of group-specific mobilty needs and demands on transportation systems of the future from the perspective of adolescents in rural areas

Der ländliche Raum ist durch geringe BewohnerInnen- und Siedlungsdichte charakterisiert. Österreichs Regionen sind weitgehend von diesen Strukturen geprägt. Flächendeckende öffentliche Verkehrsnetze und ausreichende Versorgungsangebote fehlen häufig. Mobilitätsgarant im ländlichen Raum ist ein eigenes motorisiertes Fahrzeug. Diese Abhängigkeit bedingt Ungleichheiten bei der Mobilitätsteilhabe und folglich Abhängigkeiten von anderen Personen. Vor allem Jugendliche werden durch diese Abhängigkeiten in ihrer Mobilität eingeschränkt.

Eine exemplarische Darstellung der Mobilitätsbedürfnisse im Alltag von Jugendlichen im ländlichen Raum soll eine Einschätzung der Potenziale und Maßnahmen für die Verbesserung der Chancengleichheit in der Mobilitätsteilhabe liefern. Ziel ist Chancengleichheit im ländlichen Raum. Ergebnis des Projektes ist es, Handreichungen für kommunalplanerische und regionalpolitische Maßnahmen sowie Mobilitätsinitiativen zu formulieren, welche aus den Prinzipien der vorgefundenen Beispiele abgeleitet werden und für ähnlich strukturierte Gemeinden angewandt werden können.

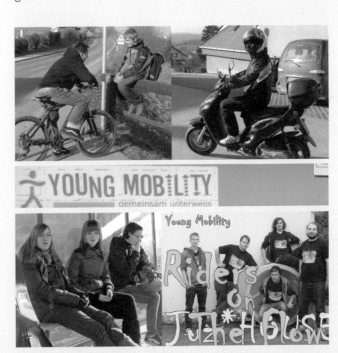

The project ECOMOB focuses on the need of every-day mobility of young men and women living in rural areas. The mobility of young men and women in the municipality of Straden, situated in south-eastern Styria, was examined – an area characterised by dispersed settlement and long distances for the inhabitants. Public transport is only existent in the form of school busses. In fact, to own a car is the only mean of transport which seems to guarantee mobility to the inhabitants. Hence, young people under the age of 18 are very much dependent on others.

The aim of ECOMOB is to create equal chances of mobility for young people; between men and women and between generations.

Furthermore, ECOMOB represents a starting point for municipal and regional planning which offers equal opportunities of everyday mobility to young men and women.

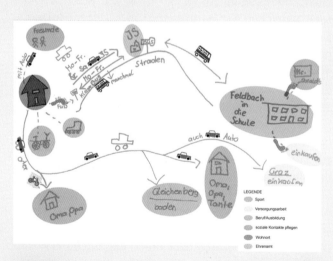

alle Abbildungen © Martina Jauschneg. zwischen. 2009 und 2011

DIⁱⁿ Eva Kail

*„Ein generelles Problem ist: Wie kommt Gender
in den Mainstream?"*

'A general problem is: how does gender cross
into the mainstream?'

Durch das Lesen feministischer Literatur während ihrer Studienzeit erhielt Eva Kail wichtige Inputs für ihre fachliche Orientierung. Arbeitsschwerpunkt, im Rahmen ihrer Tätigkeit bei der Stadt Wien, war zuerst frauengerechte Planung, später Gender Mainstreaming in Planungsprozessen. Ausgehend von einem frauenpolitischen Workshop initiierte sie eine Arbeitsgruppe, die die Ausstellung „Wem gehört der öffentliche Raum? Frauenalltag in der Stadt" organisierte. Im Anschluss daran wurde sie die erste Leiterin des neugegründeten Frauenbüros der Stadt und das erste Wohnprojekt nach frauengerechten Kriterien wurde realisiert.

Planungsansätze beschäftigten sich mit dem Thema „Vernachlässigung von unbezahlter Arbeit in der Planung". Die Erledigung von unbezahlter Arbeit kann, wie Eva Kail betont, über räumliche Qualitäten sehr wohl erleichtert werden. Mit der Gründung der Leitstelle für alltags- und frauengerechtes Planen und Bauen wurde Gender zum Querschnittsthema in vielen Planungs- und Projektierungsbereichen der Stadt Wien.

Eva Kail ist der Meinung, dass Gender Mainstreaming einen übergeordneten strategischen Ansatz darstellt, der sowohl bei der Entscheidungsabwägung, beim Prozessdesign als auch in der Planung zu berücksichtigen ist. Dieser hat großes fachliches und auch politisches Potenzial bei der Abwägung von Zielkonflikten, sofern er methodisch ernst gemeint ist und entsprechende Ressourcen zur Verfügung stehen. Seit 2010 arbeitet Eva Kail, nach der Umorganisation der Baudirektion, als Genderexpertin in der Gruppe Planung verstärkt im Mainstream.

Als grundlegendes Problem sieht Eva Kail eine gewisse Wahrnehmungsverweigerung des fachlichen Mainstreams gegenüber den Qualitäten, die durch die Auseinandersetzung mit Gender-Aspekten produziert werden. Für die Zukunft vermutet sie, dass die Anforderungen an die Planung größer und die Verteilungskämpfe um finanzielle Ressourcen gleichzeitig härter werden. Deshalb ist Gender Mainstreaming ein wichtiges Asset, um Gemeinwohlinteressen formulieren und vertreten zu können.

By reading feminist literature during her studies, Eva Kail gained important inputs for her professional orientation. In the context of her current position for the City of Vienna, she chose gender-sensitive planning as a deliberate focus in her profession. On the basis of a women's political workshop she initiated a working group and organised the exhibition 'Who owns the public space?´ Women's everyday life in the city'. Subsequently, she became the first head of the newly founded women's department and the first housing project according to women-specific criteria was realised.

Starting point of her planning approaches was unpaid work in its accomplishment, which, according to Eva Kail, can very well be supported by spatial qualities. With the Co-ordination Office for Planning and Construction Geared to the Requirements of Daily Life and the Specific Needs of Women, gender became a cross-sectoral topic in many planning- and project issues of the City of Vienna.

In Eva Kail's opinion, gender mainstreaming is like a superior strategic approach that should be considered in decision-making processes, in process design as well as in planning. It has great professional and political potential when it comes to considerations of conflicts of aims if it is meant seriously concerning the methods and if there are enough resources available. Since 2010, after the reorganisation of the department of urban planning, Eva Kail as a female expert on gender issues has increasingly been working in the mainstream.

Eva Kail somehow identifies a basic problem within the professional mainstream, regarding a refusal of the qualities produced dealing with gender aspects. She assumes that in the future requirements for planning will increase and that at the same time the struggles on the distribution of financial resources will be harsher. Therefore, gender mainstreaming is an important asset to formulate and represent common welfare interests.

von li. o. nach re. u. © Eva Kail, o. J.

1959
Geburt in Wien

1977–1984
Studium der Raumplanung an der TU Wien, Studienrichtungs- und Fakultätsvertreterin

1986
Arbeitsbeginn bei der Stadt Wien, zuerst Bezirksentwicklungsplanung für den 5. Bezirk (MA 18)

1991
Ausstellung „Wem gehört der öffentliche Raum? Frauenalltag in der Stadt" gemeinsam mit Jutta Kleedorfer

1996
vom Frauenbüro gesponserte Ausstellung mit Margarete Schütte-Lihotzky als Ehrengast

1998
Gründung der „Leitstelle alltags- und frauengerechtes Planen und Bauen" in der Baudirektion

2005
Richtlinien für eine geschlechtssensible Park- und Spielplatzgestaltung

seit 2010
Reorganisation Baudirektion, Auflösung Leitstelle, Gender Planungsexpertin in der Gruppe Planung

Zukunft
gezielter Wissenstransfer, gezielte Integration der Gender-Dimension im Smart City-Prozess

1965–1977
Schulzeit in Wien Floridsdorf, stabile, große Freundinnengruppe im Mädchengymnasium

1985
Gebietsbetreuung Ottakring

1988
Baudirektion, damaliges Dezernat für Stadterneuerung

1992
Aufbau des Frauenbüros der Stadt Wien (MA 57) als sehr junge Abteilungsleiterin, Ursula Bauer als Mitarbeiterin für die Planung

1997
Geburt von Kathi

2000
Geburt von Fanny

2002–2006
Gender Mainstreaming Pilotbezirk Mariahilf

2006–2009
50 Gender Mainstreaming Leitprojekte aus den laufenden Arbeitsprogrammen der Planungs- und Verkehrsabteilungen

2013
Handbuch „Gender Mainstreaming in der Stadtplanung und Stadtentwicklung"

Frauen-Werk-Stadt I

Frauen-Werk-Stadt I

Bearbeitungszeitraum Project Period

1992–1997

Ort Location

Donaufelder Straße 95–97, 1210 Wien Vienna

AusloberIn Initiators

Magistratsabteilung Frauenförderung und Koordinierung
von Frauenangelegenheiten der Stadt Wien (MA 57) gemeinsam mit der Magistratsabteilung Stadtteilplanung
und Flächennutzung (MA 21), Stadtentwicklung und Stadtplanung (MA 18) und Wohnbauförderung (MA 50)
Municipal Department Promotion and Co-ordination of
Women's Issues together with the Municipal Department
District Planning and Land Use, Urban Development and
Planning and Housing Promotion

ProjektpartnerInnen Project Partners

Städtebaulicher Entwurf Urban Design: Franziska Ullmann
Architektinnen Architects: Elsa Prochazka,
Gisela Podreka, Lieselotte Peretti
Freiraumplanung Open Space Planning: Maria Auböck
Kunst am Bau Art on the Construction Site: Johanna Kandler
Jury-Vorsitz Jury Chairwoman: Kerstin Dörhöfer
Ehrenvorsitz Honorary Chair: Margarete Schütte-Lihotzky
Bauträger Developer: Wiener Wohnen, Wohnbauvereinigung
für Privatangestellte

Einordnung Key Words

Städtebauliches ExpertInnenverfahren basierend auf den
Kriterien für alltags- und frauengerechtes Planen und Bauen
Urban planning experts' procedure based on the criteria for
everyday-life- and women-oriented planning and building

Die Erleichterung von Haus- und Familienarbeit, die För-
derungen nachbarschaftlicher Kontakte und ein Woh-
numfeld, das ein hohes subjektives Sicherheitsgefühl vermittelt, waren zentrale Anliegen des Modellvorhabens.
1993/94 initiierte die Magistratsabteilung Frauenförderung und Koordinierung von Frauenangelegenheiten der
Stadt Wien den Wettbewerb, basierend auf den Kriteri-
en eines alltags- und frauengerechten Wohnbaus. Das
Projekt erzeugte in seiner Entstehungsphase hohes me-
diales Interesse, auch waren die Akzeptanz seitens der
AnrainerInnen und die Nachfrage nach den Wohnungen
überdurchschnittlich groß. Es hatte damals eine wichtige
Signalfunktion: einerseits um die Teilhabe von Frauen im
Städtebau deutlich zu erhöhen, andererseits um das Bewusstsein für die Facetten einer alltagsgerechten Planung
zu stärken. Dazu zählen einladende Eingangssituationen,
Gänge mit Aufenthaltsqualität, Wohnungsgrundrisse, die
auf die Anforderungen der unterschiedlichen Lebenspha-
sen flexibel reagieren können, Kinderwagenabstellräume
auf jedem Stockwerk sowie eine helle und übersichtliche
Tiefgarage. Eine Evaluierung bestätigte 1997 eine hohe
Wohnzufriedenheit. Heute ist die Frauen-Werk-Stadt I
mit rund 360 Wohnungen nach wie vor Europas größtes,
von Architektinnen nach den Kriterien eines alltagsgerechten Wohnbaus errichtetes Bauvorhaben. Auch zwei
Jahrzehnte nach Bezug erweist sich der städtebauliche
Ansatz als robust und tragfähig.

© Johannes Faber, 2000
© Johannes Faber, 2000
© Johannes Faber, 2000
© Margherita Spiluttini, 1999

The facilitation of house and family work, the encouragement of neighbourly contacts and a living environment which produces a high subjective sense of security were the central concerns of this pilot project. In 1993/94 the City of Vienna, Municipal Department Promotion and Co-ordination of Women's Issues, initiated a competition based on the criteria of everyday life and women-oriented housing. The project attracted much media interest during its development and also the neighbours' acceptance and the demand for flats were above the average numbers. It had a strong signalling effect, on the one hand to considerably increase the share of women in urban development and, on the other hand, to raise awareness on the facets of everyday-life-oriented planning. This comprises inviting entrances, hallways with qualities of stay, flat layouts with the ability to react flexibly to the requirements of different life phases, storage rooms for push chairs in every storey, as well as a bright and clearly arranged underground car park. An evaluation from 1997 confirmed the high housing satisfaction. Today, the Frauen-Werk-Stadt I with 360 flats still represents Europe's biggest housing project built by female architects on the basis of everyday-life-oriented housing criteria. Two decades after the move-in the urban development approach still proves to be robust and sustainable.

Masterplan Masterplan

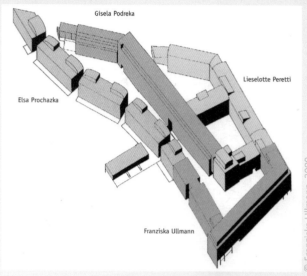

Gisela Podreka
Lieselotte Peretti
Elsa Prochazka
Franziska Ullmann

© Franziska Ullmann, 2009

„Soziale Augen" 'social eyes'

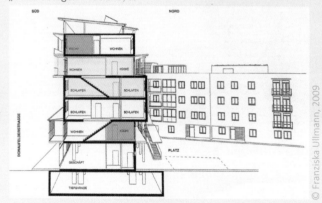

© Franziska Ullmann, 2009

Eine Wohnung für jede Lebensphase A flat for each phase of life

© Franziska Ullmann, 2009
© Margherita Spiluttini, 1999
© Margherita Spiluttini, 1999
© Margherita Spiluttini, 1999

© Grundriss Elsa Prochazka, Grafik Andrea Neuwirth

© MA 18, o. J.

DIⁱⁿ Jutta Kleedorfer

„Gemeinsinn geht immer vor Eigennutz."

'Sense of community always comes before selfishness.'

Sagt man Jutta Kleedorfer „Das geht doch nicht", setzt dies bei ihr den Motor erst so richtig in Gang. Diesen Motor zu bremsen, ist nur schwer möglich. Er ist hartnäckig, unermüdlich und schlagkräftig. Ein Zurückschalten gibt es eigentlich nicht. Mit diesen Eigenschaften konnte sie viele Projekte unterstützen, wie etwa die Ballspiel- und Sportanlage am Gaudenzdorfer Gürtel, das Fluc (Veranstaltungsort, Kunst- und Klangraum am Wiener Praterstern), den Mädchengarten, die Skaterhalle und Jugendtreffs. Die Palette ist bunt. Vor einem Projekt fragt sie sich, wer davon profitiert. Macht sie ein Projekt für Mädchen, versucht sie, das nächste für eine andere Gruppe zu machen. Egal ob männlich oder weiblich, jung oder alt. Für Jutta Kleedorfer bedeutet Gender mehr als nur Frauenpolitik. Vielmehr steht im Mittelpunkt: Wer braucht was? Was gönnen wir uns gegenseitig?

Während der Ausbildung und im Beruf sträubte sich Jutta Kleedorfer gegen die vorherrschenden Normen. Sie beschreibt sich als ein „Bürgerkind mit Lust auf Revolution und Liebe zur Gerechtigkeit". Anfang der 1970er-Jahre kam sie von Deutschland nach Österreich, wo sie auf der BOKU Wien Landwirtschaft studierte. Im 2. Abschnitt studierte sie Raumplanung an der TU Wien. Hier war sie froh, endlich nicht nur Trachtenanzüge zu sehen.

Mit dem Studienabschluss (1978) begann die Arbeit als Freiberuflerin. Ende der 1980er-Jahre änderte sich jedoch alles schlagartig: Geburt der Tochter, Lehrauftrag an der BOKU Wien und Anstellung beim Magistrat der Stadt Wien. Anfang der 1990er-Jahre folgte gemeinsam mit Eva Kail die Ausstellung „Wem gehört der öffentliche Raum? Frauenalltag in der Stadt".

Geändert hat sich schon einiges. Für Jutta Kleedorfer ist Gender Mainstreaming mit anderen Schwerpunkten notwendiger als noch vor 15 Jahren. Mittlerweile ist Jutta Kleedorfer Projektkoordinatorin für Mehrfachnutzung und in die Magistratsabteilung 18 – Stadtplanung und -entwicklung eingegliedert. Ihr größtes Anliegen ist die Realisierung von Projektideen. Das tut sie ohne Weisungsrechte und eigene finanzielle Mittel.

If someone says 'You can't do that' to Jutta Kleedorfer, it is the moment when her engine really gets started. Then, it is difficult to stop her insistent, tireless and powerful motor, there is no gearing down. With this temper, she already supported many projects such as the creation of a ball games area fields at the Gaudenzdorfer Gürtel, the Fluc (an event venue, art and sound space at Praterstern, Vienna), a Girls' Garden, a skate area and meeting point for teenagers. Before Jutta Kleedorfer starts a project, she always asks herself who is going to benefit from it. When she carries out a project for girls, she tries to work for another group in following projects. It does not matter to her whether the target group is male or female, young or old. For Jutta Kleedorfer, gender mainstreaming means more than women's policies. The focus rather lies on: Who is in need of what and what do we grant each other?

During her education and in her professional life she resisted against prevailing standards. She describes herself as a 'bourgeois child with the desire for revolution and love of justice'. At the beginning of the 70s, she moved from Germany to Austria to study agriculture at BOKU Vienna. Later, she changed to TU Vienna, where she concluded her studies in urban and regional planning.

After finishing her studies (1978) she started to work as a freelancer. At the end of the 80s, however, everything suddenly changed with the birth of her daughter, a teaching assignment at the BOKU Vienna and an employment at the municipality of the City of Vienna. At the beginning of the 90s, the exhibition 'Who owns the public space? Women's everyday life in the city'. was carried out.

Since then, things have changed. To Jutta Kleedorfer, gender mainstreaming is necessary in a different way than 15 years ago. Currently, she is project coordinator of 'Mehrfachnutzung' (multiple use) and integrated in the Viennese Municipal Department 18 – Urban Development and Planning. She has no budget for the projects and no authority, but she is using all her energy to help implementing them.

1953
geboren in Wuppertal, Nordrhein-Westfalen, Deutschland

1971
Abitur; Beginn des Studiums der Sozialpädagogik in Wuppertal, Neuss, Köln

ab 1972
Studium der Landwirtschaft an der BOKU Wien

ab 1975
2. Studienabschnitt an der TU Wien: Raumplanung; parallel zum Studium Mitarbeit bei ÖKISTA, Wien (StudentInnenreisebüro)

1978
Abschluss DI^{in} an der TU Wien

ab 1979
freiberufliche Tätigkeit als Raumplanerin in div. Raumplanungsbüros

1988
Monographie „Über Höfe + Dächer – verborgenes Grün in der Stadt"

1989
Johannas Geburt Beginn Lehrauftrag an der BOKU Wien (bis 2002)

1984
Heirat mit Peter Kleedorfer, seine Tochter Veronika wuchs bei ihnen auf

1990
Beginn Anstellung beim Magistrat Wien

1991
Ausstellung „Wem gehört der öffentliche Raum? Frauenalltag in der Stadt" mit Eva Kail

Mitte 1990er-Jahre
Projekte mit Arbeitsgruppen zu unterschiedlichen Themen

1998
Ernennung: Projektkoordinatorin für Mehrfachnutzung, mit Sitz in der Baudirektion

2002
Projektkoordination „einfach-mehrfach" in MA 18 eingegliedert

Projektkoordinatorin für Mehrfachnutzung

Project Coordinator for Multiple Use

Bearbeitungszeitraum
Seit 1998

Ort
Wien

Auftraggeberin
Stadt Wien

ProjektpartnerInnen
Unterschiedliche, je nach Projekt

Einordnung
Diversity-Projekte

Project period
Since 1998

Location
Vienna

Principal Investigator
City of Vienna

Project Partners
Diverse, according to project

Key Words
Diversity projects

In einer dichten Stadt treffen die verschiedensten Ansprüche auf engstem Raum aufeinander. Vor allem Kinder und Jugendliche finden nicht ausreichend Spiel-, Bewegungs- und Freiraum. Ziel von „Mehrfachnutzung" war und ist es, v.a. die Potenziale der stadteigenen Flächen für weitere InteressentInnen zu öffnen – z. B. Schulhöfe und Schulsportanlagen nachmittags, samstags, sonntags und in den Ferien – sowie zeitweise ungenützte Flächen (Baulücken) anderer GrundbesitzerInnen temporär bespielbar zu machen: „Zwischennutzung". Die Projektkoordination hilft bei der Vermittlung zwischen den AkteurInnen und deren Interessen. Sie unterstützt die Personen, Initiativen und Gruppen bei der Durchführung ihrer Projektideen.

Entwicklung

Seit der Beauftragung 1998 haben sich die Anforderungen geändert: von Outdoor- zu ganzjährig nutzbaren Indoor-Angeboten als Ergänzung zu Parkbetreuung & Co. Sie ermöglichen Kindern und Jugendlichen Dinge auszuprobieren, die sie nicht unter einer breiten Beobachtung, wie im Park, machen wollen. Nebenbei lassen sich wetterunabhängig Veranstaltungen durchführen.

Mädchengarten: Die Betreuung erfolgt durch tilia (Büro für Landschaftsplanung) und die Parkbetreuung Simmering.
Girls' Garden: The supervision is carried out by tilia (office for landscape planning) and the park attendants of Simmering.

In a densely populated city, various (conflicting) demands meet each other in the narrowest spaces. Especially children and adolescents have problems in finding places to play as well as other leisure activities. The aim of 'multiple use' is in particular to open the potentials of city-owned areas to special groups of interest. For example, granting access to schoolyards and school sport facilities during the afternoon, weekends and holidays as well as to temporarily unused places (space between buildings) of other owners – 'Zwischennutzung' (in temporary use). The project coordination helps in the mediation of interests between different actors. The persons, initiatives and groups receive help with the implementation of their project proposals/ideas.

Development

Since the commissionning in 1998, the requirements have changed: from outdoor to year-round indoor offers in addition to park attendants & co. These enable children and adolescents to try out other activities they would not try out under broad observation like in a park. Besides, indoor offers are not dependent on the weather.

Skatearea 23: Betreut wird die Halle im 23. Bezirk vom „Verein zur Förderung der Skatekultur". Die Skateboarding Schule bietet mehrmals wöchentlich Kurse an. Skatearea 23: The area is managed by the 'Association for the Promotion of Skate Culture'. The school offers several courses a week.

Fluc: Architekt Stattmann plante eine Bebauung mit Containern über der ehemaligen FugängerInnenunterführung am Praterstern. Fluc: The architect Stattmann planned a construction with containers on the former pedestrian underpass at the Praterstern.

ACTiN-Park Hirschstetten: Die Schule ohne Zaun und Mauer als offene Quartiersinfrastruktur. ACTiN Parc Hirschstetten: The school without fence and walls as an open neighbourhood infrastructure.

alle Abbildungen © MA 18 – Stadtplanung und Stadtentwicklung, o.J.

DIⁱⁿ Dr.ⁱⁿ Bente Knoll

„Welche Vorstellungen einer gerechten Gesellschaft liegen dem eigenen Handeln zugrunde?"

'Which perceptions of a just society underlie one´s own actions?'

Schon vor als auch während des Studiums – z. B. in einem sogenannten Frauentutorium, wo Frauen ihre Situation als Frauen im technischen Studium thematisieren – wurde Bente Knoll im Feld der feministischen Planung aktiv. 1998 gründete sie mit zwei Architekturstudentinnen den Arbeitskreis „Frauen in der Planung". Die Gruppe – 10 bis 15 Frauen – traf sich alle zwei Wochen mittwochabends zum Lesen von Texten, zur Vorbereitung von Exkursionen und um die eigene Situation als Frauen zu reflektieren. Nach dem Studium beschäftigte sich Bente Knoll ganz bewusst zunächst nicht mehr mit dem Thema „Gleichberechtigung", sondern war im Projektmanagement tätig. Jedoch kehrte sie wieder zur Thematik „Gender und Planung" zurück. Seit 2004 führt Bente Knoll ihr „Büro für nachhaltige Kompetenz B-NK GmbH".

Für sie spielt das Berufliche im Privaten eine sehr große Rolle. Die eigenen Vorstellungen und Überzeugungen über Geschlechterverhältnisse seien sowohl im eigenen Alltag wie auch im Beruf zu finden. Fakt ist, ihrer Meinung nach, dass es immer die persönliche Auseinandersetzung braucht. Es stimmt sie zufrieden, dass 95 % der Projekte und Arbeit unmittelbar mit Gender- und Diversity-Aspekten zu tun haben. Dennoch herrschen in vielen gesellschaftlichen Bereichen nach wie vor ungleiche Verhältnisse, wie auch schon vor 10 Jahren. Hier gab es wenige Veränderungen.

Dass Frauen und Männer nicht in gleichen Ausbildungsrichtungen studieren und in manchen ingenieurwissenschaftlich-technischen Studienrichtungen der Frauenanteil immer noch unter 10 % liegt, sieht sie als Problem. Von feministischen Planerinnen wurden im Laufe der Zeit die Strategie des Gender Mainstreaming in die Planung „übersetzt" sowie Gender-Aspekte in unterschiedlichen planerischen Themenfeldern herausgearbeitet. Hauptgrund hierfür sei der Vertrag von Amsterdam und die Implementierung von Gender Mainstreaming in verschiedene gesetzliche Grundlagen.

Before and during the studies Bente Knoll was active in feminist planning in a so-called 'Frauentutorium' – where women discuss the issue of being a woman in technical studies. In 1998, she and two female students of architecture, from her studies initiated the group called 'Frauen in der Planung' – women in planning. The group of 10–15 women met every two weeks – on Wednesday evenings – to read texts, prepare excursions and reflect their situation as women. After her studies, Bente Knoll decided not to deal with the topic of equal rights any more, leaving the issue aside for a certain time. She came back to this subject and started an independent career. Since 2004, Bente Knoll holds her own 'Büro für nachhaltige Kompetenz B-NK GmbH' – Consultancy for Sustainable Competence.

Her professional life plays a major role in her private life. To her, the personal agenda and own convictions on gender issues can be found as much in daily life as in profession and it is a fact that an individual approach is always necessary. However, in many social fields unequal conditions remained unchanged and still are as they were 10 years ago. In her position it is a problem that women and men are not choosing the same branches of study and that in some engineering and technical fields of study women are still underrepresented (with less than 10 %).

To lead a business company for over 10 years and to be able to cover 95 % of projects and work directly with the topic of gender and diversity aspects is pleasing Bente Knoll.

In the last decades, feminist planners worked on the implementation of gender mainstreaming and gender aspects related to different planning topics. The main reason for this was the Treaty of Amsterdam as well as the implementation of gender mainstreaming in various legal frameworks.

1992–2000
Studium der Landschaftsplanung und -pflege an der BOKU Wien. Diplomarbeit „Parzellenhöfe in Zwischenbrücken" (Betreuerin Gerda Schneider)

1998
Gründung des Arbeitskreises „Frauen in der Planung" später „Planwerkerinnen"

2001–2009
Redakteurin der „Koryphäe — Medium für feministische Naturwissenschaft und Technik"

2004
Selbstständigkeit; Gewerbeberechtigungen: Ingenieurbüro für Landschaftsplanung und Unternehmensberatung, später Handel

2004–2006
Dissertation am Institut für Verkehrsplanung und Verkehrstechnik zum Thema „Verkehrs- und Mobilitätserhebungen. Einführung in Gender Planning", Fakultät für Bauingenieurwesen, TU Wien (Betreuer Hermann Knoflacher)

2008
Pflichtlehrveranstaltung zu Gender Studies an der Technisch-Naturwissenschaftlichen Fakultät der Johannes Kepler Universität Linz

2012/13
Personalwachstum in der Firma von einer Teilzeitkraft (11/ 2011) auf sieben Teilzeitkräfte (09/2013)

24.05.1994
Geburt von Sohn Jens

24. – 27.05.2001
Kongress von Frauen in Naturwissenschaft und Technik an der TU Wien

2003–2004
Lehrgang „Mainstreaming Gender und Diversity in modernen Organisationen"; Abschluss: zertifizierte Gender- und Diversity-Beraterin

2005
Lehrveranstaltungen an der TU Wien (in den ersten Jahren gemeinsam mit Sonja Hnilica); Teilnahme an der Summerschool der Universität Graz „Karrierestrategie für Nachwuchswissenschafterinnen"

2010
Lehrbuch „Gender Studies in den Ingenieurwissenschaften" (gemeinsam mit Brigitte Ratzer); Entwicklung der GartenBox (gemeinsam mit Ralf Dopheide)

Österreich Unterwegs 2013/14

Austria On Its Way 2013/14

Bearbeitungszeitraum

April 2013–November 2014

Ort

Innerstädtische Bezirke in Wien, Großraum Graz, Großraum Eisenstadt, Defereggental in Osttirol und Waldviertel

Auftraggeber

Bundesministerium für Verkehr, Innovation und Technologie (bmvit)

Einordnung

Qualitative Erhebungen zur Mobilität von Menschen, die im Alltag Wege für und mit anderen Personen zurücklegen

Project Period

April 2013–November 2014

Location

Inner-city districts in Vienna, Greater Graz, Greater Eisenstadt, Defereggental in East Tyrol and Waldviertel

Principal Investigator

Federal Ministry for Transport, Innovation and Technology (Bmvit)

Key Words

Qualitative surveys on the daily routine mobility of people who give support to others

Begleitend zur österreichweiten Mobilitätserhebung „Österreich unterwegs 2013/14" führt Bente Knoll und ihr Büro für nachhaltige Kompetenz vertiefende qualitative Erhebungen zur Mobilität von Menschen durch, die im Alltag Wege für andere und mit anderen Personen zurücklegen.

Dabei stehen Fragen nach den alltäglichen Wegeketten und den (individuellen) Mobilitätsentscheidungen im Zusammenhang mit dem Gesamtarbeitsalltag im Zentrum. Zu den Untersuchungsgebieten zählten, als dichter innerstädtischer Raumtyp (mit einer dichten Versorgung an öffentlichen Verkehrsmitteln), der 4. bis 9. Wiener Gemeindebezirk, als typisch städtischer Raumtyp in Österreich, die beiden Landeshauptstädte Graz und Eisenstadt – jeweils mit deren Einzugsgebieten. Als ländliche Raumtypen wurden einerseits das Defereggental in Osttirol (Hochgebirgstal) und andererseits das Waldviertel in Niederösterreich (periphere Lage) ausgewählt.

In Form von Einzel- und Fokusgruppen-Interviews wurden Personen, die unbezahlte Betreuungs- und Versorgungsarbeit für kleinere Kinder, Kinder und Jugendliche, sowie für ältere Menschen übernehmen, befragt. Lebenswelten sind einem dynamischen Wandel unterworfen und die befragten Personen leben in unterschiedlichsten Formen zusammen. Die Spannbreite reicht hierbei von einem „traditionellen" Lebensentwurf („Mutter-Vater-Kind") über die „Ein-Kind-Familien" bis hin zu den bislang in der Mobilitätsforschung wenig beachteten „Patchworkfamilien" und „multilokalen Familien" – das sind Personen in einer Paarbeziehung mit Kind(ern), die zumindest teilweise im gleichen Haushalt leben.

Accompanying the Austria-wide mobility survey 'Österreich unterwegs 2013/14' Bente Knoll and her Consultancy for Sustainable Competence lead in-depth qualitative surveys on the daily routine mobility of people who give support to others.

The surveys focus on everyday trips and the (individual) mobility decisions in connection with the entire workday. Study areas were the districts 4 to 9 in Vienna as examples of dense inner-city area type (with a dense supply of public transport) and the two provincial capitals of Graz and Eisenstadt, representing a typical urban area type in Austria – each with its catchment area. As rural area types, the Defereggental in East Tyrol (high mountain valley) and the Waldviertel in Lower Austria (peripheral location) were selected.

People who care for small children, children and young people as well as elderly people without getting paid were interviewed in single- and group focus interviews. Living environments are subject to a dynamic change and the persons interviewed are living together in a variety of forms. The spectrum ranges from a 'traditional' family concept ('mother-father-child') to 'one-child families' and also includes 'patchwork families' and 'multi-local families' – (a couple with child(-ren) living at least partially in the same household) which were mostly ignored in mobility studies up until now.

Mobilität ist ein vielschichtiges Phänomen
Mobility is a multidimensional phenomenon

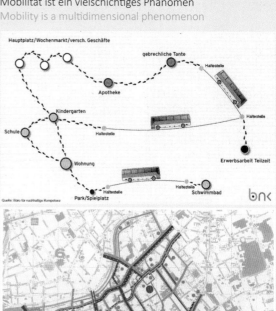

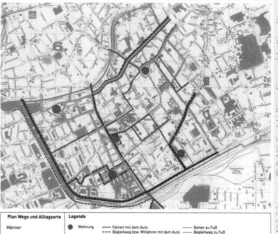

alle Abbildungen © B-NK GmbH Büro für nachhaltige Kompetenz, o. J.

© BABF, 2004

Mag.ª DIin Dr.in Theresia Oedl-Wieser

„Es hängt sehr viel vom Engagement
einzelner Personen ab."

'Many things depend on the commitment
of individuals.'

Seit Anfang der 1990er-Jahre befasst sich Theresia Oedl-Wieser mit Fragen der Frauen- und Geschlechterforschung im ländlichen Raum in Österreich. Während des Soziologie- und Landwirtschaftsstudiums (Universität Wien, BOKU Wien) fiel ihr auf, wie gering das Interesse am Thema im Allgemeinen war: „Und das hat mich irrsinnig gestört. Dadurch bin ich auf das Thema gekommen und wollte mehr dazu erfahren und mir etwas dazu erarbeiten." Dies war der Anstoß zu ihrer Arbeit zu ruralen Frauen- und Geschlechterfragen sowie Gender Mainstreaming in der ländlichen Entwicklung. „Die Ungleichheit zwischen Frauen und Männern hat strukturelle Gründe", weiß Theresia Oedl-Wieser. Sie interessiert sich in ihrer Arbeit für die Ursachen der geringen Präsenz von Frauen in agrar-, regional- und kommunalpolitischen Gremien. „Wenn man die Ursachen für Ungleichheiten analysiert und aufzeigt, können diese nach und nach abgebaut werden."

Besonders wichtig ist ihr ein gutes Netzwerk, um den Austausch von Ideen zwischen Wissenschaft, NGOs und Regionalinitiativen zu fördern und Lobbyarbeit zu ermöglichen. „Meine Motivation, zum Thema Gender Mainstreaming zu arbeiten, verläuft wellenartig." Ähnlich schwankt auch das Interesse der Öffentlichkeit, welches durch Aktivitäten hochgehalten werden muss – „dann kommen vielleicht Zeiten, in denen Gender Mainstreaming wieder mehr Wertschätzung erfährt." Es mangelt an Dokumentation und Evaluierung der vielen Aktivitäten, die bereits umgesetzt wurden. „Es besteht Sensibilisierungsbedarf auf allen hierarchischen Ebenen und in vielen Handlungsfeldern, damit die Strategie des Gender Mainstreamings reifen kann."

„Für das Privatleben ist der Begriff ‚Gleichstellung' geeigneter", stellt die Mutter zweier Kinder für sich fest. „Es ist ein schönes Gefühl, wenn es gelingt, dass man – gemeinsam mit dem Partner – Familie und Berufsleben miteinander vereinbaren kann. Und da müssen alle zusammenhalten."

Since the beginning of the 1990s, Theresia Oedl-Wieser has been working on women's and gender issues in rural areas in Austria. During her studies of sociology and agriculture (University of Vienna, BOKU Vienna) she noticed a generally low interest in this topic: 'This bothered me enormously, hence I wanted to learn more about the topic and develop something on it.' It was the beginning of her work on rural women's and gender issues as well as gender mainstreaming in rural development. 'The disparity between women and men has structural reasons', Theresia Oedl-Wieser points out. In her professional life she has focused on the reasons for the low representation of women in agricultural and local politics. 'By analysing and identifying the reasons for disparities we can reduce them gradually.'

Of special importance, in her opinion, is a good network to promote the interchange of ideas between science, NGOs and local initiatives and to allow lobbying work. 'My motivation for the work with gender mainstreaming is wave-like.' The public interest similarly alternates. It needs to be kept high by activities because 'then gender mainstreaming may hopefully again experience periods of high appreciation.' There is a lack of documentation and evaluation on the numerous activities already implemented and 'it needs much work to increase sensitivity on all hierarchical levels and in many fields of action to let the strategy of gender mainstreaming mature.'

'For private life the word 'equality' fits better', says the mother of two children. 'It is a good feeling when you can successfully combine family and work life together with a partner. Therefore, in this point, we all have to stick together.'

1963
Geburt

bis 1983
Schulausbildung

1987–2000
Studium der Soziologie und Publizistik an der Universität Wien (Belegung von Seminaren zu Frauen- und Geschlechterforschung)

ab 1993
Wissenschaftliche Mitarbeiterin der Bundesanstalt für Bergbauernfragen

1994–2009
Food and Agriculture Organisation/European Commission on Agriculture – Working Party of Women and the Family in Rural Development (Expertin, Board Member, Vice Chair)

2003
„Gleichstellungsorientierte Regionalentwicklung" (Interdisziplinäres Projekt)

2010
„Landwirtschaftliche Betriebsleiterinnen in Österreich" (Forschungsbericht Nr. 62) Leader Mid-Term-Evaluierung

2011
„Umsetzung von Gleichstellung von Frauen und Männern in den ländlichen Entwicklungsprogrammen in Österreich" (Facts&Feature 48)

1990–1992
Österreichische Bergbauern- und Bergbäuerinnenvereinigung (NRO)

1992–1993
Vertragsassistentin an der BOKU Wien (Institut für Agrarökonomie)

1997
Geburt von Tochter Franziska + „Emanzipation der Frauen am Land" (Forschungsbericht Nr. 40)

2000
Promotion an der BOKU Wien

2006
„Frauen und Politik am Land" (Forschungsbericht Nr. 56)

2008
„Gender Issues" (Sonderband des Jahrbuches der Österreichischen Gesellschaft für Agrarökonomie; gemeinsam herausgegeben mit Ika Darnhofer)

ab 2012
Geschäftsführung der Österreichischen Gesellschaft für Agrarökonomie

2013
Mitveranstalterin der Tagung „Frauen am Land – Potenziale und Perspektiven" an der BOKU Wien

Ausgewählte Publikationen zu ruraler Frauen- und Geschlechterforschung

Selected Publications on Rural Women and Gender Studies

Herausgeberin
Forschungseinrichtung Bundesanstalt für Bergbauernfragen, Wien, Österreich

Einordnung
Ländliche Entwicklung, Regional Governance, Gender Mainstreaming, Rurale Frauen- und Geschlechterforschung

Editor
Federal Institute for Less-Favoured and Mountainous Areas, Vienna, Austria

Key Words
Rural Development, Regional Governance, Gender Mainstreaming, Rural Women- and Gender Issues

Frauen und Politik am Land

Das Hauptergebnis der Studie zeugt davon, dass Frauen in der ländlichen politischen Öffentlichkeit deutlich unterrepräsentiert sind und kaum höhere Positionen in politischen Institutionen und Gremien innehaben. Dies geschieht trotz des entscheidenden Beitrages, den Frauen durch ihre Arbeit in der Landwirtschaft, durch die innerfamiliäre Versorgungsarbeit und ihre ehrenamtliche Arbeit für das soziale und wirtschaftliche Leben in ländlichen Regionen leisten.

Women and politics in rural areas

The main findings of this study were that only very few women hold positions in political institutions and key bodies and are underrepresented in rural public politics. This, despite the fact that – through their work in agriculture, care work for their family and voluntary work for society – women play a crucial role in the rural economy and the social life of villages and regions.

OEDL-WIESER, Theresia (2006): Frauen und Politik am Land. Forschungsbericht Nr. 56 der Bundesanstalt für Bergbauernfragen. Wien.

Chancengleichheit im Rahmen des Österreichischen Programms für die Entwicklung des ländlichen Raumes
Die Schriftenreihe „Facts & Feature", Nr. 28, behandelt im Rahmen der Mid-Term-Evaluierung des Österreichischen Programms für die Entwicklung des ländlichen Raumes (PELR) 2003 die zusätzliche nationale Querschnittsfrage „Chancengleichheit im ländlichen Raum: Die Lebens- und Arbeitssituation der Frauen im ländlichen Raum".

Gender Equality within the Framework of the Austrian Programme for Rural Development
Within the framework of the mid-term-review by the Austrian Programme for Rural Development (RDP) 2003, Facts & Feature No. 28 deals with the additional national cross-cutting question 'Equal opportunities: the living and working conditions for women in rural areas'.

Emanzipation der Frauen auf dem Land
Ausgangspunkt des Forschungsberichtes sind Veränderungen in Österreich durch die Öffnung der Ostgrenzen, die Globalisierung der Wirtschaft, den EU-Beitritt – und deren Auswirkungen auf Frauen in ländlichen Regionen.

Emancipation of Women in Rural Areas
Given the substantial and far-reaching changes that have taken place in recent years in Austria – opening of the eastern borders, globalization of the economy, EU accession – and their impacts on rural areas, it is time to ask about how concerned women in rural areas are by these changes.

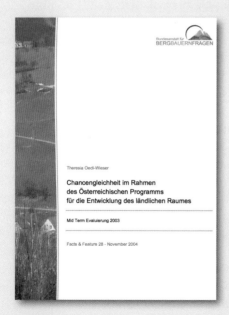

OEDL-WIESER, Theresia (2004): Chancengleichheit im Rahmen des Österreichischen Programms für die Entwicklung des ländlichen Raumes. Mid-Term-Evaluierung 2003. Facts & Feature Nr. 28 der Bundesanstalt für Bergbauernfragen. Wien.

OEDL-WIESER, Theresia (1997): Emanzipation der Frauen auf dem Land. Eine explorative Studie über Ambivalenzen und Lebenszusammenhänge. Forschungsbericht Nr. 40 der Bundesanstalt für Bergbauernfragen. Wien.

DIⁱⁿ Hanna Posch

An der Universität begann Hanna Posch, sich mit feministischer Planung zu beschäftigen. Dort besuchte bzw. organisierte sie verschiedene Lehrveranstaltungen zu diesem Thema. Außerdem war sie Teil einer Gruppe mit dem Namen „flugs" (feministische Landschaftsplanerinnen unterwegs), welche unterschiedliche Texte bzw. die Thematik an sich diskutierte. Der Begriff Gender Mainstreaming tauchte für Hanna Posch erst im Arbeitsleben auf, wo sie dann auch einige Projekte dazu durchführte.

Die Gender-Perspektive spielt auch in ihrem Privatleben eine große Rolle. Für sie war Gleichberechtigung sowohl privat als auch beruflich immer schon ein wichtiges Thema.

Für Hanna Posch hat Gender Planning im Vergleich zur feministischen Planung den Vorteil, dass sich sowohl Frauen als auch Männer damit beschäftigen. Es ist nicht nur Frauensache. Gender Mainstreaming ist ihrer Meinung nach inzwischen ein Thema mit weitaus mehr Akzeptanz geworden. An ihrem Arbeitsplatz – im Büro – ist Gender Mainstreaming in der Planung immer schon ein Thema bzw. ein gewollter Arbeitsschwerpunkt gewesen, weil es einfach zum Team bzw. zu den einzelnen Persönlichkeiten dazugehört.

Es ist schwierig, die zukünftige Entwicklung von Gender Mainstreaming und Diversity einzuschätzen. Hanna Posch hat das Gefühl, dass Gender Mainstreaming für die meisten Menschen greifbarer ist als der Begriff Diversity und dass es deshalb auch leichter ist, damit zu arbeiten. Für die Weiterentwicklung im Bereich Gender Mainstreaming sieht Hanna Posch zwei parallel laufende Strömungen: einerseits eine Standardisierung, also ein echtes Mainstreaming, und andererseits einen „Backlash", also Personen, die das Thema bereits abgenutzt und unspannend finden und sich nicht mehr damit beschäftigen wollen. Noch ist nicht abzuschätzen, wohin es sich entwickeln wird.

„Der Begriff Gender Mainstreaming ist für viele Menschen in den letzten Jahren greifbar geworden."

'In recent years, the concept of gender mainstreaming has become more tangible for many people.'

It was at university that Hanna Posch started to deal with the issue of feminist planning. There she attended and organised various lectures on this topic. Moreover, she was also part of a group called 'flugs' (feminist landscape planners on their way), within which different texts and topics were discussed.

The first time Hanna became acquainted with the term gender mainstreaming was when she started working and carried out some projects on this topic after finishing her studies. In her private life, the gender perspective also plays an important role. Equality issues have always been of great importance to her.

To Hanna Posch, the advantage of gender mainstreaming in comparison to feminist planning is that both women and men deal with it. It is not only women's business. In her view, gender mainstreaming is being more and more accepted. At Hanna Posch's office, gender mainstreaming has always been a main focus in planning because it belongs to a deliberate work priority and is part of the team or rather part of every single person in the office.

It is difficult to assess the future development of gender mainstreaming and diversity. However, Hanna Posch thinks that for most of the people gender mainstreaming is more tangible than diversity, which makes it easier to work with it.

Generally, she sees two parallel lines in the future development of gender mainstreaming: on the one hand a standardisation, therefore a real mainstreaming of the topic, and on the other hand a backlash. This means that there will be people who think that the topic is already worn-out and hence refuse to work with it any further. Nevertheless, she believes that it cannot yet be estimated how gender mainstreaming is going to develop and how people are going to deal with it in future.

bis 1985
Kindheit und Schulzeit in Kärnten; Übersiedlung nach Wien

1985 bis 1994
Studium der Landschaftsökologie/ Landschaftsplanung; Beschäftigung mit feministischer Theorie und Praxis im Rahmen von „flugs" (feministische Landschaftsplanerinnen unterwegs)

1996
Projektarbeit an der Universität von Barcelona

1997
Gründung von PlanSinn gemeinsam mit 5 KollegInnen; Geburt Leonie

1999
Übersiedlung nach Wolkersdorf im Weinviertel (mit Großeltern im selben Haus)

2000
Geburt Simon (berufliche Auszeit ca. 1 Jahr)

2006
Gender Mainstreaming Pilotbezirk Mariahilf

seit 2008
lokale Kulturarbeit im forumschlosswolkersdorf

2011
Handbuch „Gender Mainstreaming – leicht gemacht. Praxistipps für mehr Gleichstellung im Magistrat"

2015
Dialog zum Wiener Gleichstellungsmonitor

laufend
(Weiter)Entwicklung interner Gender- und Diversity-Projektreflexionen

Gender Mainstreaming –
Pilotbezirk Mariahilf

Gender Mainstreaming – Pilot District Mariahilf

Bearbeitungszeitraum
2005–2007

Ort
Wien

Auftraggeberin
Stadt Wien

ProjektpartnerInnen
Geschmacksache Medienwerkstatt
Zuckerstätter-Semela Renate
Müller Carla – Illustrationen
tilia – Büro für Landschaftsplanung

Project period
2005–2007

Location
Vienna

Principal Investigator
City of Vienna

Project Partners
Geschmacksache Medienwerkstatt
Zuckerstätter-Semela Renate
Müller Carla – illustrations
tilia – office for landscape planning

Im öffentlichen Raum prallen täglich die verschiedenen Interessen von NutzerInnen aufeinander. Alle im Planungsbereich Tätigen müssen daher in ihren Entscheidungen ständig die Interessen dieser NutzerInnengruppen abwägen. Gender Mainstreaming kann dafür eine wichtige Grundlage bieten.

PlanSinn moderierte dazu einen Entwicklungsprozess im 6. Wiener Gemeindebezirk. Dieser Prozess wurde von der Leitstelle für alltags- und frauengerechtes Planen und Bauen initiiert und von SachbearbeiterInnen und WerkmeisterInnen aus sechs Magistratsabteilungen und der Bezirksvertretung getragen. Wesentlich war, mit den technischen ExpertInnen gemeinsam Methoden für die Anwendung im Alltag zu entwickeln. Im Rahmen des Prozesses wurden wirksame Maßnahmen, die z. B. die Bedingungen für FußgängerInnen verbessern, gesetzt. Dabei wurden die Auswirkungen der Maßnahmen auf verschiedene NutzerInnen genau beleuchtet. Zur Vermittlung der Ergebnisse produzierte PlanSinn die Broschüre „Stadt fair teilen" (Leitstelle für alltags- und frauengerechtes Planen und Bauen, Stadtbaudirektion Wien, 2007).

Public spaces are spaces in which the different needs and interests of users necessarily and continuously collide. People involved in planning are therefore constantly challenged to reconcile the interests of the different user groups. Gender mainstreaming is an important decision-making tool in this field.

PlanSinn facilitated and moderated a gender mainstreaming pilot development process in Vienna's 6th district. This process was initiated by 'Co-ordination Office for Planning and Construction Geared to the Requirements of Daily Life and the Specific Needs of Women' and supported by experts and senior staff from six municipal departments and the district authorities. A key objective was to elaborate appropriate methods for the practical implementation of the concept in everyday life. A number of effective measures, e.g. for improving conditions for pedestrians, were realised and carefully analysed with regard to their impact on the different users. PlanSinn produced the brochure 'Stadt fair teilen' (fair shared city) to disseminate the results and findings (Leitstelle für alltags- und frauengerechtes Planen und Bauen, Stadtbaudirektion Wien, 2007).

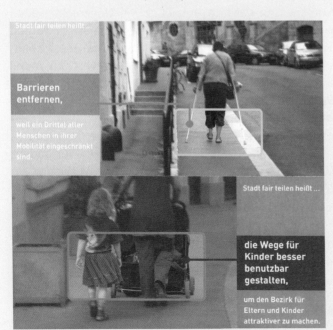

Stadt fair teilen heißt ...

Barrieren entfernen,

weil ein Drittel aller Menschen in ihrer Mobilität eingeschränkt sind.

Stadt fair teilen heißt ...

die Wege für Kinder besser benutzbar gestalten,

um den Bezirk für Eltern und Kinder attraktiver zu machen.

Stadt fair teilen heißt ...

Sicherheit im Verkehr für alle gewährleisten,

weil 60% der Unfälle mit tödlichem Ausgang FußgängerInnen betreffen.

Stadt fair teilen heißt ...

Sitzplätze im öffentlichen Raum schaffen,

weil Möglichkeiten zum Ausrasten für ältere Menschen besonders wichtig sind.

Die kritische Aufarbeitung und Auseinandersetzung mit dem Thema „Benachteiligung (durch Planung)" wurde schon früh ein wesentlicher Bestandteil der alltäglichen Professionsarbeit für Gerda Schneider. Gegen Ende ihres Studiums, 1979, begannen die ersten Lehrveranstaltungen, die sich mit dem Thema Frauen und Planung auseinandersetzten. Die Suche nach dem Platz der Frauen, nach der Vision des gestärkten Miteinanders und der Chancengleichheit z. B. am Arbeitsplatz, die Frage nach sozialräumlicher Organisation, welche gleichberechtigte Handlungsfreiräume ermöglicht, sowie der differenzierte Blick waren Fragen, die Gerda Schneider stets begleiteten und prägten.

Früh begann sie sich zu engagieren. Als jahrelanges Mitglied der Arbeitsgemeinschaft „Feministische Freiraumplanung" arbeitete sie unter anderem daran, feministische Diskurse in das Verständnis von Planungen zu übersetzen. Sowohl in ihrer Familie als auch später im Studium und Beruf, waren autonome Frauen, die ihren eigenen Weg gehen, prägend für sie. Als eine ihrer Visionen im Hinblick auf Gender Mainstreaming nennt Gerda Schneider die Entwicklung einer Gesellschaft, die Diskriminierung gänzlich aufgibt sowie Ungerechtigkeiten – die heute in Form von Strukturen organisiert werden – sieht und diese bewusst verändert. Eine Gesellschaft, in der unterschiedliche Gruppen gleichwertigen Anteil am gesellschaftlichen Leben haben und für sich eigene Perspektiven entwickeln. Als eines ihrer Lebensmottos beschreibt Gerda Schneider ihre eigene Position als die einer Außenseiterin, weil sie Veränderungen von Lebensqualität insbesondere für Frauen, aber auch für andere Gruppen erreichen möchte; gleichzeitig verbindet sie diese Position mit einem in der Mitte der Gesellschaft stehenden, zentralen und autonomen Standpunkt, in dem sie sich verortet.

© Gerda Schneider, 2014

O. Univ. Prof.^{in} Dr.^{in}-Ing.^{in} Gerda Schneider

*„Der Platz der Frauen:
zentral und autonom."*

*'The place of women:
central and autonomous.'*

For Gerda Schneider, the critical reflection on discrimination caused by planning soon became an essential aspect of her professional work. Towards the end of her studies (1979), lectures considering women in planning disciplines were implemented in the curricula of the study programme she enrolled. The search for the place of women, along with the vision of a 'strengthened reciprocity' and equal opportunities – e.g. at the workplace the question of a socio-spatial organisation which allows equal spheres of activities, as well as a differentiated view and perspective – accompanied and influenced her.

Already very early, she got involved at different levels. As a member of the 'Arbeitsgemeinschaft Feministische Freiraumplanung', she worked on transferring the feminist discourse to the understanding of landscape planning. Autonomous women – in her family, colleagues at the university and in professional life – were her inspiration and influenced her personal development. As one of her visions regarding gender mainstreaming, Gerda Schneider highlights the importance of the establishment of a society without discrimination, a society which would identify the structures causing discrimination and change them. Such a society would provide different groups of people with equal access to social life and would allow them to develop individual perspectives. On the one hand, Gerda Schneider positions herself as an outsider, because she wants to achieve a change in the quality of life – especially for women but also other groups of people –, and on the other hand, she sees her standpoint as a central, autonomous one, situated in the middle of the society where she positions herself.

1973–1979
Studium der Landschaftsplanung an der Gesamthochschule Kassel

1980–1992
Planungsgruppe „Landschaft und Stadt" Saarbrücken

1982–2008
Mitglied der Architektenkammer des Saarlandes

1989
Promotion Dr.in-Ing.in

1990
Mitglied Arbeitsgemeinschaft „Feministische Freiraumplanung"

1992–1994
Leiterin des Amtes für Grünanlagen und Forsten der Landeshauptstadt Saarbrücken

1994
Berufung zur Professorin für Landschaftsplanung an der BOKU Wien

2002
Leitung des Institutes für Landschaftsplanung an der BOKU Wien

2005–2008
Vorsitzende der Schiedskommission BOKU Wien

seit 2006
Mitglied der Departmentleitung des Departments für Raum, Landschaft und Infrastruktur an der BOKU Wien

seit 2009
Mitglied BOKU-Senat

Lebensqualität von Frauen und Männern im ländlichen Raum im Sinne von Gender Mainstreaming

Life Quality of Women and Men in Rural Areas regarding Gender Mainstreaming

Bearbeitungszeitraum Project Period
Jänner 2006 – Februar 2008 January 2006 – February 2008

Ort Location
Gemeinden Unterweißenbach im Mühlkreis OÖ), Kirchberg an der Pielach (NÖ)
Municipalities of Unterweißenbach im Mühlkreis (Upper Austria), Kirchberg an der Pielach (Lower Austria)

Auftraggeber Principal Investigator
Bundesministerium für Land- und Forstwirtschaft,
Umwelt und Wasserwirtschaft
Institut für Landschaftsplanung, BOKU Wien
Federal Ministry of Agriculture, Forestry,
Environment and Water Management
Institute of Landscape Planning
Department of Landscape, Spatial and Infrastructure
Sciences, BOKU Vienna

Projektmanagement Project management
Gerda Schneider, Peter Kurz
ProjektpartnerInnen Project partners
Regionalplanungsgemeinschaft Pielachtal,
Regionalverband Mühlviertler Alm, Marktgemeinde
Unterweißenbach und Marktgemeinde
Kirchberg an der Pielach
Regional Planning Committee Pielachtal, Regional
Association Mühlviertler Alm, municipality
Unterweißenbach and municipality
Kirchberg an der Pielach

Landschaftsplanerisches Projekt zur Lebensqualität von Frauen und Männern im ländlichen Raum im Sinne von Gender Mainstreaming am Beispiel der Gemeinden Unterweißenbach im Mühlkreis (OÖ) in der Region Mühlviertler Alm und Kirchberg an der Pielach (NÖ) in der Ökoregion Pielachtal.

Die unterschiedlichen Lebensalltage von Frauen und Männern sind vielfach der Ausgangspunkt für ungleiche Lebenschancen. Die zwei Gemeinden im ländlichen Raum wurden exemplarisch hinsichtlich ihrer Lebensqualitäten für Frauen und Männer anhand der Erschließungs-, Siedlungs- und Landbewirtschaftungsstrukturen detailliert dargestellt und kontextualisiert. Die Gemeinden stellten Handlungs- und Umsetzungsebenen von Planungen, Programmen und letztlich von Leitbildern dar, die national, regional und kommunal formuliert werden konnten.

Die Partizipation von Frauen und Männern, Bäuerinnen und Bauern, Jungen und Alten erfolgte durch Aktions- und Arbeitstage, Stammtische, themen- und zielgruppenorientierte Workshops sowie in Leitfadengesprächen im Rahmen der Forschungstätigkeit vor Ort. Die Arbeit zur Durchführung der partizipativen Veranstaltungen sowie die Vermittlungsarbeit in zahlreichen informellen Gesprächen wurden von den jeweiligen lokalen ProjektkoordinatorInnen getragen.

Eine kleinräumige Kuppenlandschaft bestimmt das Wirtschaften in der Region Mühlviertler Alm. A small-scale hilly terrain determines the maintainace of the landscape in the Mühlviertler Alm Region.

Landscape planning project on the life quality of women and men in rural areas regarding gender mainstreaming, represented by the two examples of the municipalities of Unterweißenbach im Mühlkreis (Upper Austria) and Kirchberg an der Pielach (Lower Austria).

Different daily life routines of women and men are often the reason for unequal life chances. Gender mainstreaming reveals structures which induce these unequal life chances. On the basis of their structures of accessibility, settlement and agriculture, the two municipalities were exemplarily described, analysed and contextualised in detail with regard to their life qualities for women and men.

The municipalities presented their planning strategies and planning practice containing programmes and concepts, which were ultimately to be formulated on a national, regional and communal level. The participation of men and women, female and male farmers, young and old people took place by days of action and working day meetings, theme and target workshops as well as guided conversations within the framework of the research on site. The organisation of participative events as well as mediation work in numerous informal conversations were carried out by the respective local project coordinators.

Beispiel einer Mental Map aus den Erhebungen: „eingespielter" SeniorInnen-Alltag in der Gemeinde. Example of mental map from collected data: 'usual' seniors-daily routine.

Tätigkeiten Activities
- Einkäufe Purchases
- Ausflüge: Wandern, Essen, Kultur usw. Exkursions: hiking, meal, culture etc.
- Besuche Visits
- Urlaub Holidays

Wahrnehmungsanalyse: Alltag mit Haus- und Subsistenzwirtschaft in der Gemeinde. Perception analysis: daily routine with housekeeping and subsiste economy among the community.

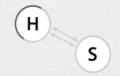

Ackerbau ist im Pielachtal auf die Gunstlagen im Talboden beschränkt. In the Pielachtal arable farming is limited to the favourable areas in the valley.

Schulworkshop
School workshop

Begehung in Unterweißenbach
On-site visit

Aktionstag in Unterweißenbach
Day of action

Thematische Stammtischgespräche. Thematic discussions at regular meeting.

alle Abbildungen © Kurz, Peter; Schneider, Gerda; Heilmann, Christoph; Jauschneg, Martina; Petrovic, Sonja; Reifeltshammer, Stefan; Scharmann Ingrid

© Andreas W. Rausch, 2012

DIⁱⁿ Susanne Staller

Auf der Suche, wohin das Studium der Landschaftsplanung sie führen würde, kam Susanne Staller im Rahmen einer Lehrveranstaltung von Jutta Kleedorfer zu „Frauen an der BOKU Wien", zum Feminismus. Sie fühlte sich während des Aufwachsens als Frau nie benachteiligt, da sie immer die Unterstützung und das Vertrauen ihrer Mutter hatte, der es wichtig war, dass sie als Frau einen Beruf erlernt. Erst durch die genauere Auseinandersetzung mit dem Thema sind ihr die Unterschiede und die Benachteiligungen in manchen Bereichen bewusster aufgefallen. Feministische Planungszugänge hatten im Büro „tilia" von Beginn an einen zentralen Stellenwert. Dazu wurde schon in der BOKU Wien-Frauengruppe eine gemeinsame Position erarbeitet und nun in der Projektarbeit weiterentwickelt. Auf für Frauen und Mädchen parteiliche und feministische Projekte folgte auch die Auseinandersetzung mit Gender Mainstreaming, welches sie als Chancengleichheit versteht. Ziel sollte ein Kontinuum sein, in dem es keine Einteilung in Frauen und Männer und dazugehörige gesellschaftliche Rollen braucht, sondern sich jeder/jede selbst autonom verorten kann, ohne einen gesellschaftlichen Nachteil davon zu haben. Für Susanne Staller ist das Thema Gender heute viel weniger aufgeladen als früher. Damals wurde dieses schnell kritisiert und gesagt, „Es gibt keine Ungleichheiten zwischen Männern und Frauen" oder „Das ist halt von Natur aus so". Heute traut sich niemand mehr, das Thema anzugreifen, es wird dadurch aber auch oft nicht so ernst genommen.

In der öffentlichen Diskussion ist das Thema heute weniger präsent, da die Meinung herrscht, in diesem Bereich wurde schon genug verändert. Aufmerksam zu sein für neue Facetten und an der Veränderung der Geschlechterverhältnisse zu arbeiten ist wichtig.

„Jeder Mensch sollte die Chance haben, sich in einem Kontinuum zwischen Mann und Frau selbst zu verorten."

'All human being should have the opportunity to position themselves in a continuum between male and female.'

In the search where the studies of landscape planning may take her, Susanne Staller got to know women dealing with feminism in planning during a course at the BOKU Vienna, led by Jutta Kleedorfer. While growing up, she never felt discriminated against as a woman, because she always had the support and trust of her mother, who thought that it was important for her as a woman to acquire a profession. However, she realised differences and noticed discrimination in specific areas, only when she started to deal with the topic in detail. At her workplace, in the 'tilia' office, a feminist planning approach has always had great significance and gender has always been a central topic. Common positions on the topic had already been developed earlier in the women's group of the BOKU Vienna and were to be enhanced in projects. Women-based, feminist projects were succeeded by a confrontation with gender mainstreaming, which Susanne Staller sees as synonymous with the equality of opportunities.

Its goal should be a continuum without the need of an exact division in women, men and associated social roles. Everyone should position oneself autonomously without social disadvantage. To Susanne Staller, the gender topic today appears less charged than in the past. Back then, people criticised frequently and said, 'There are no differences between men and women' or 'That's the way it is because it is natural'.

Today, no one dares to touch the topic, consequently, however, it is not taken so seriously anymore. In public discussions, the topic is less present today because of the opinion that there have been enough changes achieved in this field. However, it is important to be attentive for new facets and to continue working on a change in the gender ratio.

von li. o. nach re. u. © Barbara Gungl, 2014; GB*21, 2014; Susanne Staller; tilia- büro für landschaftsplanung, o. J.

1970
Geburt in Wien; aufgewachsen auf den oberen Wieden

Bergsteigen

Wandern im Wienerwald

1988
Matura; dann BOKU Wien: Studium Landschaftsökologie und Landschaftsplanung „flugs" (feministische Landschaftsplanerinnen unterwegs)

Österreichische HochschülerInnenschaft BOKU Wien Studienrichtungsvertretung, Kommissionsarbeit, Fachschaftsliste

1994/1995
Barcelona Erasmus

1995–1999
Selbstständigkeit im WG-Zimmer

1996
Diplomingenieurin für Landschaftsplanung; Schrebergarten

1997–2007
Mädchengarten; Verein Wirbel (5 Frauen); BOKU Wien-LVA

1999
Einsiedlerplatz – geschlechtssensible Planung Gründung „tilia" – büro für landschaftsplanung (3 Frauen) Stadt-Fair-Teilen

Gender-City-Planspiel

2002
Geburt von Laurenz

2005
Geburt von Matteo

2008–2011
Nachbarschaftsgarten Roda-Roda-Gasse

2012
GB*21 Gebietsbetreuung Stadterneuerung

2014
„tilia" wird 15

149

Mädchengarten

Girls' Garden

Bearbeitungszeitraum

1997–2007

Ort

Wien Simmering

AuftraggeberInnen

Magistratsabteilung Frauenförderung und
Koordinierung von Frauenangelegenheiten der Stadt Wien
(MA 57); Magistratsabteilung Bildung und
außerschulische Jugendbetreuung der Stadt Wien (MA 13)

ProjektpartnerInnen

Parkbetreuung Balu&DU; Verein Wirbel; tilia – Büro
für Landschaftsplanung; Szene Wien; Stadt Wien

Project period

1997–2007

Location

Simmering, Vienna

Principal Investigator

Municipal Department Promotion and
Co-ordination of Women's Issue and Education;
Municipal Department Out-of-School Activities for
Children and Young People of the City of Vienna

Project Partners

Park attendant Balu&DU; Association 'Wirbel';
tilia – office for landscape planning;
Szene Wien; City of Vienna

Der Mädchengarten im elften Wiener Gemeindebezirk ist ein Ort, der nur für Mädchen und Frauen zugänglich ist. Er verdeutlicht die Bedeutung eigener Freiräume für Mädchen und Frauen im Hinblick auf die Entwicklung ihrer räumlichen und sozialen Kompetenzen. Durch diesen sozial sicheren Ort werden völlig andere Tätigkeitsspektren von Mädchen sichtbar, als sie im öffentlichen Raum zu beobachten sind.

Die ursprüngliche Idee beinhaltete eine schrittweise Öffnung für alle, bei der jedoch Mädchen gegenüber Buben einen Vorsprung bekommen sollten durch vorhergehende Veränderungen und Planung des Gartens mit Jugendarbeiterinnen und Landschaftsplanerinnen. Für die Förderung der Identifikation und Aneignung sollte die Ausstattung des später öffentlich zugänglichen Gartens gemeinsam mit den Mädchen bestimmt und verwirklicht werden. Sobald jedoch Buben in den Garten gelassen wurden, war wieder die allgemeine Situation hergestellt, in der patriarchale Verhältnisse herrschen, und die Mädchen verhielten sich genau so wie draußen. Daher wurde der Garten für eine Mädchen- und Frauenöffentlichkeit zugänglich gemacht. Dieser steht nun für Mädchen einmal in der Woche begleitet durch die Freizeit- und Parkbetreuung Simmering („Balu&DU", ein ehrenamtliches Mentorenprogramm zur Förderung von Kindern im Grundschulalter) – zur Verfügung oder ist für Frauengruppen und Mädchen mit volljähriger Begleitperson zugänglich und nutzbar.

Der Mädchengarten ist als Pilotprojekt ein wichtiger Bestandteil der feministischen Mädchenarbeit in Wien.

The Girls' Garden in Vienna's eleventh district is a garden open to girls and women only. It demonstrates how important spaces open to girls and women are for the development of their spatial and social competences. In this socially secure place, girls show a different spectrum of activities than in public space.

The original idea was to open the place to everybody after the girls had been able to change and plan the garden with the help of female youth workers and landscape planners in order to give them a head start over the boys. For the promotion of the identification and appropriation, the facilities of the later public garden were to be planned and built together with the girls. The girls' ideas and suggestions for changes were included in the planning from the beginning. However, as soon as boys came into the garden, the usual situation where patriarchal circumstances prevail was reestablished and the girls acted like in public. Therefore, the garden was made accessible to girls and women only. It is now open to girls once a week under the supervision of the park attendants in Simmering (Balu&DU) and can be used by groups of women or girls with adult supervision.

As pilot project the Girls' Garden is an important project revealing the feminist girls' work in Vienna.

alle Abbildungen © Verein Wirbel, 1998–2000

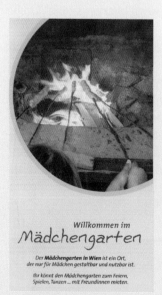

Willkommen im
Mädchengarten

Der **Mädchengarten in Wien** ist ein Ort,
der nur für Mädchen gestaltbar und nutzbar ist.

Ihr könnt den Mädchengarten zum Feiern,
Spielen, Tanzen … mit Freundinnen mieten.

DIⁱⁿ Dr.ⁱⁿ Heide Studer

Heide Studers Auseinandersetzung mit Geschlechterfragen begann mit der autonomen Frauenbewegung, bei der gemeinsam geredet, gelacht und neue Lebenswege abseits des gesellschaftstypischen Frauenbilds entwickelt wurden. Diese Erkennung der eigenen Diskriminierung war für Heide Studer aber auch mit Schmerz und Abgrenzung verknüpft. Während ihrer Studienzeit setzte sie sich im Rahmen eines Frauen-Lesekreises und im Zuge ihrer Diplomarbeit weiter mit dem Thema auseinander und versuchte mit der Unterstützung anderer, Lehrveranstaltungen und Vorträge zu organisieren.

Heide Studer empfindet Projekte und Konzepte zum Thema Gender Mainstreaming teilweise als sehr starr, weil sie sich häufig mit dem spießen, was auf wissenschaftlicher Ebene über Geschlechterzusammenhänge diskutiert wird. Aus der wissenschaftlichen Perspektive ist Geschlecht in weitesten Teilen gesellschaftlich hergestellt und es gibt durchaus mehr als zwei Geschlechteridentitäten. Dem steht im Gender Mainstreaming, eine starke Verankerung einer klar definierten Zweigeschlechtlichkeit gegenüber. Für Heide Studer ist Geschlecht fließend, eine eindeutige Festschreibung von Geschlechteridentitäten ist nicht notwendig. Deshalb stellt das Büro „tilia" den Geschlechteraspekt bei den Projekten nicht mehr in den Vordergrund, sondern bearbeitet ihn durchgängig auf allen Ebenen.

Aktuell sieht Heide Studer eine große Spanne zwischen der wissenschaftlichen Entwicklung, Gender Mainstreaming sowie der gelebten Realität. Es gibt zwar heutzutage mehr Freiheiten hinsichtlich der eigenen Identität, parallel dazu verstärkt sich jedoch der Trend der Geschlechtermarkierung über den Kommerz. Deshalb arbeitet Heide Studer beruflich wie auch privat an einer stetigen Veränderung der Geschlechterverhältnisse.

„Gender Mainstreaming ist ein notwendiger Schritt, um Geschlechtergerechtigkeit in der Breite herzustellen."

'Gender mainstreaming is a necessary step to produce gender equality on the wide scale.'

Heide Studer's confrontation with gender issues began with the autonomous women's movement, among which women talked with each other and laughed together while developing and inventing new life paths besides the typical societal female image. The cognition of her own discrimination, however was also always connected to pain and isolation. During her studies at university, she dealt with this topic within a women's reading circle and also in the context of her master's thesis. Together with other students, she further tried to organise lectures and speeches at her faculty.

Heide Studer regards projects and concepts dealing with the topic of gender mainstreaming as quite inflexible. She opines that they do not match the discourse on gender relations conducted at the scientific level. According to the scientific perspective, gender is primarily a product of society and there are clearly more than two gender identities. This perception contrasts with the way of seeing the dualism of gender as it is conceived in gender mainstreaming concepts. Heide Studer perceives gender as something floating: there is no need for a clear identification of gender identity. Therefore, the office 'tilia' does not emphasise the gender aspect in its projects, but continuously deals with it on all levels.

Currently, Heide Studer sees a major gap between the scientific development, gender mainstreaming and the lived reality. Nowadays, although there is more freedom regarding identities, there is an intensified tendency to mark gender via commerce. Therefore, Heide Studer is working on a constant change in gender relations as much in her professional as in her private life.

1965
Geburt: „Kein Bub!"

1984
Umzug nach Wien, Mitwirkung in der autonomen Frauenbewegung – „Wir werden nicht als Mädchen geboren, wir werden dazu gemacht."

Ende 1980er-Jahre
Auseinandersetzung mit Frauenthemen in der Landschaftsökologie-Studienrichtungsvertretung, Diskussionsgruppe „flugs" (feministische Landschaftsplanerinnen unterwegs)

1990/91
Verfassen der Diplomarbeit zu Frauenräumen in Vorarlberg

1991
Familiengründung und Umzug nach Mödling

ab 1993
Umsetzung des feministischen Zugangs in der professionellen Tätigkeit, Projekte, Lehre (Frauenprojekte, integrierter Geschlechterblick, Gender Mainstreaming-Projekte)

Ende 1990er-Jahre
Gründung des Büros „tilia" und des Vereins „Wirbel"

2012
Dissertation als Sozialanthropologin abgeschlossen: „Urbane Praktiken von Mädchen und Frauen in Marokko"

2014
Interdisziplinäre und länderübergreifende Lehre

Zukunft
Nord-Süd-Begegnungen zu Raumherstellung und Geschlechterpraktiken

Schulfreiräume und Geschlechterverhältnisse

Open Spaces in Schools and Gender Relations

Bearbeitungszeitraum Project Period
Mai 2005 – März 2007 May 2005 – March 2007

Ort Location
Wien (zwölf Schulen), Graz (fünf Schulen), Deutschfeistritz (eine Schule), Gleisdorf (eine Schule), Hartberg (eine Schule)
Vienna (twelve schools), Graz (five schools), Deutschfeistritz (one school), Gleisdorf (one school), Hartberg (one school)

FördergeberInnen Financial Support
Fonds Gesundes Österreich, Bundesministerium für Bildung, Wissenschaft und Kultur, Frauenbüro der Stadt Wien, Stadt Graz, Land Steiermark
Fonds Gesundes Österreich, Austrian Federal Ministry of Education, Science and Culture, City of Vienna Women's Department, City of Graz, Provincial Government Styria

ProjektpartnerInnen Project Partners
Ass.-Prof.in Mag.a Dr.in Rosa Diketmüller – Zentrum für Sportwissenschaft und Universitätssport, Universität Wien (Projektleitung), tilia – Büro für Landschaftsplanung (Projektpartnerin)
Ass.Prof. Mag. Dr. Rosa Diketmüller – Centre for Sport Science and University Sports, University of Vienna (project leader), tilia – office for landscape planning (project partner)

Das Projekt „Schulfreiräume und Geschlechterverhältnisse" beschäftigt sich mit der Frage nach den Kriterien einer gesundheitsfördernden Gestaltung von Schulfreiräumen. Schulfreiräume sind wichtige Bewegungsräume, Lernorte und Treffpunkte für Kinder und Jugendliche. Da SchülerInnen vermehrt Zeit in Schule und Nachmittagsbetreuung verbringen, gewinnen Schulfreiräume zunehmend an Bedeutung als zentrale Orte für die körperliche und die soziale Entwicklung.

Gemeinsam mit LehrerInnen und SchülerInnen werden Möglichkeiten erarbeitet, wie Mädchen und Buben zu einer bewegungsreicheren und freudvolleren Nutzung im Setting Schule angeregt werden können. Im Projekt kommen unterschiedliche Forschungsmethoden zur Anwendung, die von der Freiraumerhebung und dem Erstellen der Plangrundlagen der ausgewählten Schulfreiräume über die Nutzungserhebung (Beobachtung, Befragung, Dokumentenanalyse) und Darstellung der Daten (Nutzungskarten, qualitative Analyse) bis hin zu der Auswertung der Daten (unter anderem durch Diskussion mit externen ExpertInnen) und dem Transfer erster Ergebnisse in den schulischen Kontext (Workshop mit Gruppendiskussion usw.) reichen. Ziel des Projektes ist die Analyse der Raumnutzung von Mädchen und Buben in unterschiedlichen Schultypen. Gemeinsam werden geschlechtersensible Empfehlungen für die gesundheitsfördernde Nutzung und Gestaltung von Schulfreiräumen erarbeitet.

The project 'Open Spaces in Schools and Gender Relations' deals with questions on criteria for a health-promoting design of school yards. These are important spaces of exercise and learning as well as meeting places for children and adolescents. Due to the fact that pupils spend most of their time in school and in after-school care, school yards are getting more and more important as central spaces for the physical and social development. Together with teachers and pupils, the possibilities of a more joyful and active use of school yards were developed. The project applied different research methods, ranging from the analysis of the school yards, investigations on how pupils actually use the school yards (observation, interrogation, document analysis) and the presentation of the data (plan of the school yard's use, qualitative analysis) to data analysis (also in discussion with external experts) and the transfer of first results into the school context (workshops and group discussions). The aim of the project was to analyse the use of space by girls and boys in the different types of schools and to develop gender-sensitive recommendations for a health-promoting use and design of school yards.

© Rosa Diketmüller, 2006

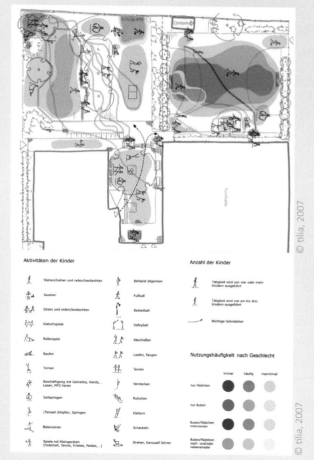

© tilia, 2007

© tilia, 2007

155

Univ.-Prof.^in DI^in Sibylla Zech

„Mehr Frauen in der Planung implizieren eine stärkere Berücksichtigung von Gender-Themen."

'More women in the profession of planning imply a greater consideration of gender issues.'

Sibylla Zech ist ein Ausnahmefall. Sie kommt gut mit den Geschlechterrollen zurecht – in einem technischen Metier wie der Raumplanung nicht selbstverständlich. Dies war nicht immer so – In ihrer Kindheit und Jugend prägten Geschlechterverhältnisse ihre Entscheidungen: Kein Realgymnasium und keine HTL, wo fast ausschließlich Burschen waren. Lieber weiter ins Gymnasium mit den anderen Mädchen gehen. Als sie für ihr Raumplanungsstudium an der TU Wien Ende der 1970er-Jahre von Vorarlberg nach Wien kam, änderte sich dies. Nur etwa 25 % der AnfängerInnen waren Frauen, beim Abschluss lag deren Quote bei 15 %.

Die Studienwahl fiel ihr leicht. Raumplanung wurde daheim schon am Mittagstisch diskutiert. Von zu Hause erhielt sie auch die notwendige Unterstützung. Während der Studienzeit befasste sie sich mit Umweltthemen, die zu dieser Zeit immer stärker in die Raumplanung implementiert wurden. Anstelle Diplomarbeit zu schreiben, wäre sie lieber in der Hainburger Au gesessen.

Nach dem Studienabschluss arbeitete Sibylla Zech als Universitätsassistentin an der TU Wien. 1991 erfolgte die Gründung des ziviltechnischen Büros „stadtland". Das Ziviltechnikerabzeichen musste extra angefertigt werden: von Ziviltechniker auf Ziviltechnikerin. Seit 2008 hat sie neben dem Büro eine halbe Professur am Department für Raumplanung inne. 50 % – perfekt für Frauen, könnte man sagen.

Mittlerweile liegt der Frauenanteil im Raumplanungsstudium bei ca. 50 %, was Sibylla Zech freut. Die Rahmenbedingungen sind gut – die Studentinnen müssten allerdings selbstbewusster auftreten. Sibylla Zech hofft, dass viele von ihnen später eine Führungsposition innehaben bzw. mit einem eigenen Büro selbstständig tätig sind. Dann würden Gender-Themen automatisch stärker berücksichtigt werden, weil Frauen eine andere Achtsamkeit haben.

Within her professional field, Sibylla Zech represents an exception. She copes very well with gender roles, which is not really a matter of course in a technical field such as spatial planning. However, this has not always been this way – during her childhood and youth, gender roles influenced her decisions: No 'Realgymnasium' and no 'HTL' with predominantly boys... she preferred to continue the 'Gymnasium', where there were other girls.

Her attitude towards this changed in 1978, when she moved from Vorarlberg to Vienna to study spatial and regional planning. At her faculty, only about 25 % of the university entrants were female and merely 15 % also accomplished their studies.

The choice of study was not difficult – spatial planning was already a topic at home during lunchtime. From home she also received the necessary support. During her study, Sibylla Zech focused on environmental topics, which became increasingly important in spatial planning at that time. Instead of writing her diploma thesis, she would have preferred to occupy the Hainburger Au.

After finishing the studies, Sibylla Zech worked as an university assistant at the TU Vienna. In 1991, the civil engineering office 'stadtland' was established. The civil engineering badge had to be manufactured especially for her – until then, it had only existed in the male version. Since 2008, she has additionally been holding a half-time professorship at the Department of Spatial Planning at the TU Vienna. 50 % – seemingly perfect for a woman.

Currently, the percentage of women studying spatial planning at the TU Vienna is about 50 %. Sibylla Zech is glad about this. The circumstances are very good – female students merely have to show more self-confidence.

Sibylla Zech hopes that many of the female students will attain leading positions or be self-employed in their own office. As a consequence, gender themes would automatically be more considered as women have a different attentiveness.

1960
Geburt Feldkirch

1978
Matura

1978
Beginn Studium TU Wien „Raumplanung"

ab 1979
Praktika in Raumplanungbüros, öffentlichen Planungsstellen

1984
Abschluss der Studiums; Diplomarbeit über Umweltverträglichkeitsprüfung

1984–1991
Univ. Assistentin TU Wien, Institut für Landschaftsplanung und Gartenkunst; Mitarbeit in Planungsprojekten verschiedener Architektur- und Raumplanungsbüros

1987
Stellvertreterin des Institutsvorstands

1991
Ziviltechnische Prüfung; Gründung ZT-Planungsbüro „stadtland", Wien – Hohenems (nunmehr Bregenz)

2008
halbe Professur TU Wien, Institut für Regionalplanung

2005
Umgründung vom ziviltechnischen Büro (ZT) „stadtland" zum Technischen Büro

GmoaBus Pöttsching

GmoaBus Pöttsching

Bearbeitungszeitraum

1999–2004, seit 2000 in Betrieb

Ort
Pöttsching

Auftraggeberin
Gemeinde Pöttsching, gefördert vom
bmvit (Bundesministerium für Verkehr,
Innovation und Technologie)

ProjektpartnerInnen
Stadtland; komobile (ehem. TRAFICO)

Project period

1999–2004, in operation since 2000

Location
Pöttsching

Principal Investigator
Municipality of Pöttsching, funded by
the bmvit (Federal Ministry for Transport, Innovation and Technology)

Project Partners
Stadtland; komobile (former TRAFICO)

Zum Einkauf, zum Arzt oder zur Ärztin, zur Schule, zum Sport – Mobilität ist Teil unseres Lebens. Vor allem Kinder und ältere Menschen haben es aber oft schwer, ohne Hilfe ihre Wege und Termine wahrzunehmen und Erledigungen nachzukommen. Meist sind sie auf Personen angewiesen, die sie mit dem Auto bringen und holen. Viele kurze Autofahrten sind daher Begleitfahrten und werden meist von Frauen übernommen. Diese Begleit- und Erledigungsfahrten nehmen Zeit und Geld des Familienbudgets in Anspruch, erhöhen das Verkehrsaufkommen, gefährden FußgängerInnen und RadfahrerInnen und belasten die Umwelt.

Der GmoaBus (Gemeindebus) bietet in Pöttsching seit 2000 Abhilfe. Ursprünglich als Modellprojekt zur Frauenmobilität geplant, wird dieser von einer breiten Bevölkerungsschicht angenommen. In die Projektplanung waren insbesondere Frauen involviert, in der Organisation und im laufenden Betrieb spielen Frauen eine führende Rolle. Der GmoaBus ist nicht nur ein wichtiges Mobilitätsangebot, er hat auch positive soziale und wirtschaftliche Effekte.

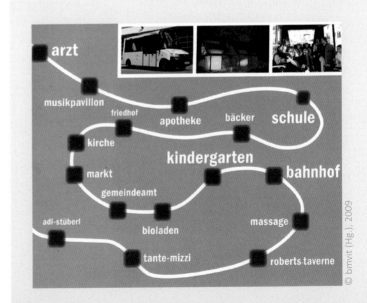

Mobility is central to our lives – whether it concerns going to school, doing sports, visiting the doctoror going to a shop. Especially children and elderly people have difficulties to manage their appointments without help. Usually they depend on other persons picking them up and taking them somewhere by car. Therefore, many short rides are accompanied trips and are mostly carried out by women. These are time consuming and represent a burden to the family budget, increase the volume of traffic, threaten pedestrians and cyclists and pollute the environment. Since 2000, the GmoaBus (municipal bus) Pöttsching provides relief. Originally designed as a pilot project for women's mobility, it has been accepted by a broad sector of the population. Mainly women had been involved in the project planning and implementation and still play an important role in the operation and organisation of the project. The GmoaBus does not only represent an important mobility service, it also has positive social and economic effects.

Das GmoaBus - Lied

Hört ihr das Geratter? Hört ihr diesen Lärm?
Es kommt immer näher, es ist nicht mehr fern.
Und auf einmal steht er groß und gelb vor mir.
Nein, ich kann´s nicht glauben. Was ist das vor mir?

Es ist der GmoaBus, der gelbe GmoaBus,
der gelbe, gelbe GmoaBus.
Es ist der GmoaBus, der gelbe GmoaBus,
der gelbe, gelbe GmoaBus.

Seht ihr seine Reifen, wenn er sich bewegt?
Fährt er wieder weiter, wie die Straße bebt!
Seine großen Türen gehen auf und zu.
Was wird jetzt geschehen? Ich steig ein im Nu.

Es ist der GmoaBus, der gelbe GmoaBus, ...

Und die Damen blinzeln mich ganz freundlich an.
Ich nehm´ meinen Fahrschein, zeig´ ihn her sodann.
Kaum setz´ ich mich nieder, geht die Fahrt schon los!
Bald bin ich zuhause, ist die Freude groß.

Es ist der GmoaBus, der gelbe GmoaBus, ...

Dieses Lied wurde von SchülerInnen der Volksschule Pöttsching zum ersten Geburtstag des
GmoaBuses geschrieben und aufgeführt.

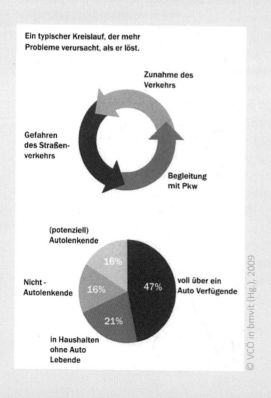

Ein typischer Kreislauf, der mehr Probleme verursacht, als er löst.

Zunahme des Verkehrs

Gefahren des Straßenverkehrs

Begleitung mit Pkw

(potenziell) Autolenkende — 16%

Nicht-Autolenkende — 16%

voll über ein Auto Verfügende — 47%

in Haushalten ohne Auto Lebende — 21%

© Lassy, 2015

DIⁱⁿ Helga Lassy

*„Die gendergerechte Planung ist eine
Selbstverständlichkeit.“*

*'Gender-sensitive planning is a matter
of course.'*

„Aller Anfang ist schwer." Diesen Satz hat schon manch einer gehört beziehungsweise selbst erlebt. Für Helga Lassy waren die Rahmenbedingungen ihres Lebensumfeldes ebenfalls nicht einfach. Sie begann Anfang der 60er- Jahre ein Architekturstudium an der TU Wien. Nach der Geburt ihrer Tochter im Jahr 1970 war es schwierig, Familie, Beruf und Studium erfolgreich in Einklang zu bringen. Durch Aufopferung, starken Willen, Zielstrebigkeit und große Liebe zu ihrem Beruf schaffte es Helga Lassy, als erste Frau in Oberösterreich ein Architekturbüro zu gründen, welches sie zu einem erfolgreichen und prosperierenden Betrieb mit 20 MitarbeiterInnen führte. Über Umwege gelangte sie in ihrer beruflichen Laufbahn zum Schwerpunkt Raumordnung. Aufgrund ihrer Tätigkeit in diesem Bereich eröffneten sich für sie neue Blickwinkel auf die Architektur selbst. „Ein gut umgesetzter Raumordnungsplan ist der Grundstein für jeden gelungenen Entwurf." Durch konsequentes Umsetzen dieser Philosophie machte sich Helga Lassy einen Namen auf diesem Gebiet und entwickelte erfolgreich Projekte im In- und Ausland. Im öffentlich geförderten Wohnbau gibt es ihrer Meinung nach einen Aufholbedarf in Bezug auf gendergerechtes Wohnen, da durch Gesetze, Richtlinien und Regulierungen der Spielraum erheblich eingeschränkt wird. Gendergerechtes Bauen war während ihrer Ausbildung noch ein unbekanntes Terrain. Aber es war schon damals notwendig, für eine gelungene Architektur auf die Bedürfnisse der NutzerInnengruppen einzugehen. Unbewusst setzt Helga Lassy diese Thematik um. In ihren Entwürfen finden Jung und Alt, Frau und Mann gleichwertig Platz. „Die gendergerechte Planung ist eine Selbstverständlichkeit". Ihrer Meinung nach ist der Begriff Gender Planning heutzutage kein reines Fremdwort mehr. Diese Thematik wird der jungen Generation an den Hochschulen vermittelt und fließt langsam, aber beständig in alle Planungsprozesse ein.

'All beginnings are difficult.' Some of us have already heard that sentence or have even experienced it. The surrounding conditions of Helga Lassy's living environment were not easy at all. In the beginning of the 60ies, she started her architectural studies at the TU in Vienna. After the birth of her daughter in 1970, it was difficult for her to reconcile work and studies with family. However, Helga Lassy succeeded in being the first woman in Upper Austria to establish an architecture office, which is now a successful business with twenty employees. After some detours in her career, Helga Lassy now focuses on spatial planning. Due to her functions in this sector, Helga Lassy has changed her perspective on architecture. 'A good implemented spatial plan is the foundation for a successful design.' Because of the consequent realisation of this philosophy, Helga Lassy could make a name for herself in this field and developed. In her opinion, there is a tremendous need to catch up on gender-sensitive habitation in publicly government-financed housing because the scope is significantly restricted due to laws, guidelines and regulations. During her education, gender-sensitive building was an unknown terrain. But even back then it was necessary to respond to the user group's needs for a successful architecture.

Helga Lassy realises this issue subconsciously. In her plans there is space for the old and the young as well as women and man. 'Gender-sensitive planning is a matter of course.' In her opinion, the term gender planning not sound like a foreign word anymore. This topic is being communicated to the young generation at the universities and will be integrated in all planning processes.

1961
Architekturstudium an der TU Wien

1969
Wiederbeginn des Architekturstudiums in Wien

1974
Abschluss des Architekturstudiums, DI^{in}

1977
Geburt von Sohn Günter
Arbeit bei Architekt Komlanz

1982
Ziviltechnikerprüfung – Beginn der Selbstständigkeit

1985
Übersiedlung in ein neues Büro mit wachsender Zahl an Angestelllten und Projekten

2010
Nominierung zum Staatspreis für den Masterplan der voestalpine

1964–1969
Heirat und Übersiedlung nach Offenbach bei Frankfurt
Studienunterbrechung
Arbeit in verschiedenen Architekturbüros

1970
Geburt von Tochter Silvia

1974–1979
Arbeit bei Architekt Haller im Wiener Architekturbüro

1979
Übersiedlung mit den Kindern nach Linz

1983
Büro in der Wohnung
1. Auftrag – Flächenwidmungsplanüberarbeitung der Gemeinde Kallham

ab 1986
Wettbewerbs-SiegerIn verschiedener Ausschreibungen z. B.: Chemie LKW-Einfahrtsgebäude mit Verkehrslogistik (1986); Gestaltung des voestalpine Masterplanes (1999); BLUE DANUBE AIRPORT LINZ Flughafenneugestaltung (2010) usw.

2014
Übergabe des Büros an Sohn – Architekt DI Günter Lassy

© Foto: Franz Pfemfert

Margarete Schütte-Lihotzky

„Architektur hat mit Gesinnung und
Weltanschauung zu tun."

'*Architecture has to do with ethos and paradigms.*'

Margarete Schütte-Lihotzky war eine der ersten Frauen der K.K. Kunstgewerbeschule (heute Universität für angewandte Kunst Wien) und die erste Frau, die den Beruf der Architektin in Österreich ausübte. Früh zeigten sich ihre Talente und sie bekam schon während ihres Studiums Preise für ihre Entwürfe. Nach dem Studium war sie in der Siedlerbewegung tätig und engagierte sich von Anfang an für die sozialen Fragen des Wohnbaus. Mit Adolf Loos zusammen plante sie Wohnhäuser. 1926 wurde sie an das Hochbauamt der Stadt Frankfurt am Main berufen. Ihr erster großer Erfolg war die Ausarbeitung der „Frankfurter Küche", welche bis heute als Prototyp der modernen Einbauküche gilt. Für die Wiener Werkbundsiedlung plante sie zwei Reihenhäuser. Unter den 32 ArchitektInnen war sie die einzige Frau. Ab 1930 waren sie und ihr Ehemann in der Sowjetunion mit der Gruppe von Experten um Ernst May tätig und versuchten neuen Städtebau zu verwirklichen. Sie mussten 1937 die Sowjetunion verlassen. Nach Paris und London fanden sie die Möglichkeit an der Akademie der bildenden Künste in Istanbul zu unterrichteten. Zwei Jahre später reiste sie nach Wien, um mit der österreichischen kommunistischen Widerstandsbewegung gegen den Nationalsozialismus aufzutreten. Sie wurden durch die Gestapo im Jahr 1941 festgenommen. Margarete kam ins Frauengefängnis nach Aichach, Bayern, aus dem sie 1945 von den US-Truppen befreit wurde. Nach dem Krieg lebte sie wieder in Wien. Wegen ihrer politischen Ansichten erhielt sie kaum öffentlichen Aufträge. Sie baute jeweils zwei Kindergärten und Wohnhäuser. In dieser Zeit engagierte sie sich vor allem für die Frauen- und Friedensbewegung. 1980 erhielt sie den Architekturpreis der Stadt Wien. Fünf Jahre später veröffentliche sie das Buch "Erinnerung an den Widerstand". Sie starb im Jänner 2002. Nach ihrem Tod wurden ihre Manuskripte "Warum ich Architektin wurde" veröffentlicht.

Margarete Schütte-Lihotzky was one of the first women at K.K. Kunstgewerbeschule (today University of Applied Arts Vienna) and therefore also one of the first female architects in Austria. Her talents manifested themselves very early and she received awards for her conceptual designs before even graduating. After completing her studies, she worked together with Adolf Loos, planning apartment buildings . It did not take long for her to achieve first success. 1926 she was assigned at the public work service in the City of Frankfurt. Margarete designed the 'Frankfurt Kitchen', which is one of her best-known creations. This kitchen is classified as the prototype for modern fitted-in kitchens. Furthermore she created two row houses for the Vienna Werkbund Housing Estate. Margarete was the only woman among 32 male architects. Before she moved to Istanbul -- to teach at the Academy of Fine Arts in 1938 – she and her husband worked in Soviet Union until 1937. Two years later, she returned to Vienna in order to support the communist resistance movement. In 1941, she was arrested by the Gestapo. She was detained in a women's prison in Aichach, Bavaria, where she was freed four years later by US troops. After the war, she returned to Vienna, however was not offered a lot of public contracts due to her political stance. However she designed two kindergartens and two residential buildings. She was engaged in the women's and peace movement. In 1980, she received an award for architecture from the City of Vienna. Five years later, Margarete released her memoirs 'Memories from the Resistance'. She died in January 2000. After her death, another book called 'Why I Became an Architect' was published.

REFERENCES:

ARCHITEKTURZENTRUM WIEN: www.architektenlexikon.at (access on 14.10.2016)

VEREIN MARGARETE-SCHÜTTE LIHOTZKY CLUB: www.schuette-lihotzky.at (access on 14.10.2016)

ZWINGL, Christine. Verein Margarete-Schütte Lihotzky Raum Wien (email on 14.10.2016)

von li. o. nach re. u. © Porträtfoto: Franz Pfemfert; Modell: Foto: Birgit und Peter Kainz / Rekonstruktion: Franz Hnizdo; Grundriss aus: Bauwelt 9/1927;
© Universität für angewandte Kunst Wien, Kunstsammlung und Archiv

23.01.1897
in Wien geboren

1915–1919
Architekturstudium

1926–1930
Frankfurt am Main
Ausarbeitung der
Frankfurter Küche

1930–1937
Sowjetunion

1932
Doppelhaus
Werkbundsiedlung

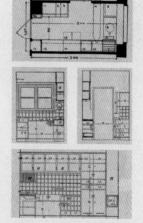

1938
Übersiedlung nach Istanbul

1940–1945
Widerstandstätigkeit,
Gefangenschaft

1980
Architekturpreis der
Stadt Wien

1985
veröffentlichte Margarete
ihre Memoiren
„Erinnerungen aus dem
Widerstand"

18.01.2000
verstorben

On Stage! Mélange | The Show Must Go On

Doris Damyanovic, Barbara Zibell, Eva Álvarez

Alle drei Ausstellungen „On Stage! – Women in Landscape_Architecture and Planning" wurden vom 3. bis 5. September 2014 anlässlich der „8th European Conference on Gender Equality in Higher Education" an der TU Wien gezeigt. Diese Konferenz, organisiert von der Abteilung Genderkompetenz geleitet von Brigitte Ratzer an der TU Wien, brachte WissenschaftlerInnen, Lehrende, VerwaltungsmitarbeiterInnen, PolitikerInnen, PraktikerInnen und StudentInnen zusammen und war eine Plattform, um über Wissenschaftskulturen, Arbeitsbedingungen in der Wissenschaft, Gender-Wissen in der Forschung, Gender-Didaktik, Karriereplanung unter Berücksichtigung von Geschlechtergerechtigkeit zu diskutieren.

Die Konferenz war ein guter (vorläufiger) Abschluss für diese internationalen Lehrkooperationen von vier europäischen Universitäten (LUH, UPV, BOKU Wien, TU Wien), die Expertinnen und geschlechtsspezifische Ansätze in Planungs- und Ingenieurwissenschaften sichtbar machen woll(t)en. Studierende der Fachrichtungen Raumplanung und Architektur haben in der Lehrveranstaltung „Gender and Diversity Aspekte in Planung und Berufsleben" im Sommersemester 2014, geleitet von Gesa Witthöft und Petra Hirschler an der TU Wien, ein Konzept für die Ausstellung On Stage! als Teil der internationalen Konferenz erarbeitet.

Die Veranstaltung diente als Bühne für inzwischen 34 Frauenporträts aus verschiedenen planungs- und ingenieurwissenschaftlichen Disziplinen – Architektur, Landschaftsarchitektur, Raumplanung, Geographie, Verkehrsplanung und Agrarsoziologie. Der Veranstaltungsort der Konferenz- das Hauptgebäude der TU Wien – am Wiener Karlsplatz – wurde zum Ausstellungsort. Einige Hörsäle wurden für diese Zeit nach ausgewählten porträtierten Frauen benannt. Die Session „Gender Studies in Engineering and Planning Faculties" ermöglichte Lehrenden und Studierenden, mit internationalen ExpertInnen konkrete Erfahrungen der Verankerung von Gender Studies in den Technik- und Planungswissenschaften in Österreich und Deutschland zu diskutieren sowie Ansätze zur Umsetzung vorzuschlagen (HOFBAUER und WROBLEWSKI, 2015). Gender-Wissen als eine wichtige Voraussetzung, um Chancengleichheit für alle in Planung und Architektur in Praxis und Forschung mitzudenken (DAMYANOVIC et al., 2014), wurde im Hinblick auf Gender-Schwerpunkte in Lehre und Forschung diskutiert. Wie z. B. Gender Awards für Qualifizierungsarbeiten mit Gender-Schwerpunkt, als Beispiel sei der Inge-Dirmhirn Preis genannt, der an Studierende seit 2006 jährlich für ausgezeichnete Master- und PhD-Arbeiten mit genderspezifischer Ausrichtung an der BOKU Wien vergeben wird. Auch über eine verpflichtende Verankerung der Gender Studies in Bachelor-, Master- und PhD-Studiengängen raumrelevanter Wissenschaften wurde nachgedacht. Konkret: Wie kann man das Thema mit persönlicher Betroffenheit mit Studierenden – Frauen wie Männern – diskutieren, z. B. auch das „Gender Wage Gap" (HOFBAUER und WROBLEWSKI, 2015). Die inter- und transdisziplinären Lehrveranstaltungen, die die On Stage! Etappen begleiteten (und ggf. zukünftig begleiten werden), sind ein wichtiger Beitrag zur Vermittlung von Gender-Wissen und Bewusstsein an Studierende, in dem sie durch die Entwicklung der Ausstellung zu mehr Sichtbarkeit von Frauen in den jeweiligen Disziplinen und zur Reflexion genderrelevanter Themen wie geschlechtergerechte Arbeitskulturen oder Projekte beigetragen haben und – so wünschen wir – weiterhin beitragen werden.

Dieses Buch ist die Dokumentation der ersten Etappe eines internationalen Projektes, das Frauen im Beruf und in ihren Disziplinen auf Dauer stärker ins Licht rücken möchte. Es zeigt die komplexen Lebensrealitäten und die Bandbreite, aber auch die Herausforderungen für Frauen in Planungs- und Ingenieurwissenschaften.

Der Vortrag der Architekturtheoretikerin Kerstin Dörhöfer (1986–2008 Professorin für Architektur und Urbanistik an der Universität der Künste Berlin) an der LUH im

On Stage! Mélange | The Show Must Go On

Doris Damyanovic, Barbara Zibell, Eva Álvarez

All three 'On Stage! – Women in Landscape_Architecture and Planning' exhibitions took place between 3 and 5 September 2014 at the '8th European Conference on Gender Equality in Higher Education' at the TU Vienna. This conference, organised by the gender competence department lead by Brigitte Ratzer at TU Vienna, has brought together female scientists, teachers, administrators, politicians, professionals and students, and was a platform for discussing research cultures, working conditions in research, gender awareness in research, gender didactics and career planning taking into account gender justice.

The conference was a successful (preliminary) conclusion to this international teaching collaboration between four European universities (LUH, UPV, BOKU Vienna and TU Vienna). The intention of which was to raise the profile of experts and gender-specific approaches to planning and engineering sciences. In the summer term of 2014, students specialising in spatial planning and architecture, on 'Gender and Diversity aspects of planning and professional life' course directed by Gesa Witthöft and Petra Hirschler of TU Vienna, developed a concept for the On Stage! exhibition as part of the international conference. The events have served as a showcase for currently 34 women portrayed in various planning and engineering sciences disciplines – architecture, landscape architecture, landscape planning, spatial planning, geography, transport planning and agricultural sociology. The conference venue – the main building of TU Vienna on Karlsplatz – served as the exhibition venue. Some lecture rooms were temporarily named after selected women who were portrayed. The 'Gender Studies in Engineering and Planning Faculties' session enabled teachers and students to discuss with international experts, specific experiences of the anchoring of gender studies in technical and planning

sciences in Austria and Germany and to propose approaches towards implementation (HOFBAUER and WROBLEWSKI, 2015). Gender awareness as an important precondition for thinking together about equal opportunities for everyone involved in planning and architecture in practice and research (DAMYANOVIC et al., 2014), was discussed with reference to significant gender-related issues in teaching and research. As an example of gender awards for qualification work with the emphasis on gender, the Inge-Dirmhirn Prize should be mentioned, awarded annually to students since 2006 for outstanding Masters' and PhD projects with a gender-specific focus at BOKU Vienna. Compulsory anchoring of gender studies in Bachelors', Masters' and PhD courses in sciences concerned with spatial planning has also been considered. Specifically: how can the issue be discussed with those personally concerned, with students – women and men – including, for instance, the gender wage gap (HOFBAUER and WROBLEWSKI, 2015).

The inter- and cross-disciplinary seminars accompanying the phases of On Stage! (both in the past and in the future), make an important contribution to the communication of gender awareness and knowledge to students since they have contributed and – as is our hope – will continue to contribute, through the development of the exhibition, to women having a higher profile in the appropriate disciplines, and on the reflection on gender-relevant issues such as gender-fair working cultures or projects.

This book documents the first phase in an international project that could draw greater long-term attention to women professionals in their disciplines. It shows the complex and diverse realities of life, but also the challenges for women in planning and engineering sciences. The lecture at LUH in November 2016 by architectural theoretician Kerstin Dörhöfer (1986–2008 Professor of Architecture and Urban Planning at University of the Arts Berlin) is an excellent opportunity to present this book to a (specialist) readership. Kerstin Dörhöfer is one of the German-speaking pioneers who has been research-

November 2016 ist ein ausgezeichneter Anlass, um das vorliegende Buch der (Fach-)Öffentlichkeit vorzustellen. Kerstin Dörhöfer ist eine der deutschsprachigen Pionierinnen, die seit den 1970er Jahren zu Themen wie „Frauen in der Architektur", „Geschlechterverhältnisse und Raumstrukturen" geforscht, publiziert und gelehrt hat (z. B. DÖRHÖFER, 1990; DÖRHÖFER et al., 1998).

On Stage! konnte bereits an der BOKU Wien durch Porträts von Frauen, die in den umfassenden Themenfeldern des Naturgefahrenmanagements arbeiten, erweitert werden. Gezeigt wurden sie im Frauenmuseum Hittisau in Vorarlberg und an der BOKU Wien 2016. Beide Ausstellungen dienten als Beitrag zum Auftakt des europäischen Netzwerks „Women Exchange for Disaster Risk Reduction" (we4DRR), das Frauen und Gender Aspekte im Naturgefahrenmanagement sichtbar machen möchte.

Frauennetzwerke und Plattformen, die die Genderperspektive in die Raum- und Planungswissenschaften einbringen, sind wichtige Instrumente, um Frauen und Gender-Themen in den ingenieurwissenschaftlichen Disziplinen zu positionieren. Die Plattform gender_arch-land an der LUH beschäftigt sich derzeit, ausgehend vom ehemaligen schweizerischen Frauennetzwerk Planung, Architektur, Frauen. (P,A,F.), mit der Geschichte, den Erfahrungen und Visionen einschlägiger Netzwerke. Die Fortsetzung der Ausstellung On Stage! kann ein weiterer Baustein sein, um die Vernetzung voranzutreiben und Geschichte zu schreiben, indem die eigene Geschichte aufgearbeitet wird.

Wenn die vorliegende Dokumentation dazu beiträgt, weitere Schritte in diese Richtung anzuregen und einzuleiten, dann ist ein wichtiges Ziel unserer Arbeit erreicht. Wir wirken gern auch weiterhin daran mit!

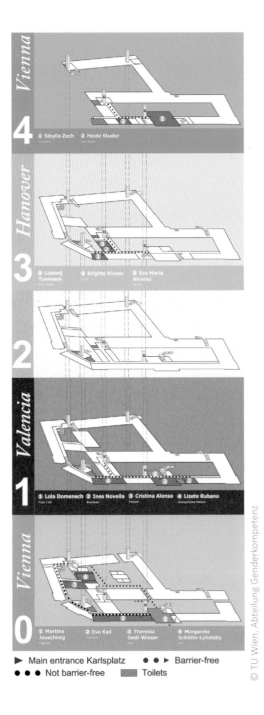

ing, publishing and teaching on issues such as 'Women in Architecture', 'gender relations and spatial structures' since the 1970s (e.g. DÖRHÖFER, 1990; DÖRHÖFER et al., 1998).

On Stage! has already been thematically extended at BOKU Vienna by portraying women working in compre-

driving the network forward and writing history as individual stories are worked through.

If this book contributes to encouraging and initiating further steps in this direction, we have achieved an important objective in our work. We look forward to further cooperation in this area!

hensive thematic areas of natural hazard management. They have been presented in the Hittisau women's museum in Vorarlberg and at BOKU Vienna in 2016. Both exhibitions contributed to kickstart the European network 'Women Exchange for Disaster Risk Reduction (we4DRR)', highlighting women and gender aspects in natural risks management.

Women's networks and platforms that introduce gender perspectives into spatial and planning sciences are an important tool for positioning women and gender issues in the engineering science disciplines. The gender_archland platform at LUH is currently occupied with recounting the story of the experiences and visions of relevant networks, starting with the former Swiss women's network on planning, architecture and women. (P,A,F.). The continuation of the On Stage! network can be further foundation for

REFERENCES:

DAMYANOVIC, Doris, HIRSCHLER, Petra, WITTHÖFT, Gesa 2014: Ein differenzierter Blick in Planung und Design (A differentiated perspective in planning and design). zoll + Österreichische Schriftenreihe für Landschaft und Freiraum. pp.21–25

DÖRHÖFER, Kerstin (Ed.). 1990. Stadt, Land, Frau: soziologische Analysen, feministische Planungsansätze, Deutsche Erstveröffentlichung. ed., Forum Frauenforschung. Kore, Freiburg

DÖRHÖFER, Kerstin, FLECKEN, Ursula, ZIBELL, Barbara 1998: Frauenforschung und Gender Studies in der Stadt- und Regionalplanung (Women's studies and gender studies in city and regional planning)., in: Vereinigung für Stadt-, Regional- und Landesplanung e.V. (SRL) (Editor), Stadtplanung und Städtebau. Positionen finden – Überzeugungen vermitteln. Eine Festschrift für Dieter Frick (Urban planning and urban construction. Finding positions – communicating convictions. A commemorative publication for Dieter Frick). Berlin, pp. 43–57

HOFBAUER, Johanna, WROBLEWSKI, Angela 2015: Equality Challenges in Higher Education. '8th European Conference on Gender Equality in Higher Education' – Content and Conclusions. Federal Ministry of Science, Research and Economy, Vienna

AutorInnen Authors

Barbara Zibell (*1955, Hanover, Germany)
is Professor of Planning Theory and the Sociology of Architecture at Leibniz Universität Hannover. She obtained her degree in Urban and Regional Planning at TU Berlin in 1980, with the first diploma thesis at this institution taking in account a women's perspective in analysing the built environment, and holds a PhD from the Institute of Technology, Zurich, which she obtained in 1994. She is President of the Forum for GenderCompetence in Architecture Landscape Planning (gender_archland), a member of GDUS network (Gender, Diversity and Urban Sustainability) and cost network genderSTE (Science, Technology and Environment). Main topics of interest are spatial planning theory, gender studies, housing and caring and sustainable development. Amongst many other memberships and affiliation, she is Regular Member of the German Academy for Spatial Research and Planning (ARL) and Board Member of the Swiss Association for Spatial Planning (VLP-ASPAN).

Doris Damyanovic (*1969, Ried/Innkreis, Austria)
is Assistant Professor of Landscape Planning at BOKU Vienna. She studied landscape planning and wrote her PhD-thesis and habilitation with the focus 'Gender-sensitive Approaches in Landscape Planning'. She has been working on gender and diversity planning topics in urban and rural areas for the last fifteen years. She is member of gender_archland, member of GDUS (Gender, Diversity and Urban Sustainability) network and European Cost network genderSTE (Science, Technology and Environment). Her research focuses on urban, rural and regional landscape planning in particular planning theories, tools and methods as well as participatory planning.

Eva M. Álvarez (*1963, Canary Islands, Spain)
has been Associate Professor at the Architectural Projects Department, Universitat Politècnica de València since 1995. She obtained her degree in architecture (with professional competences) at UPV in 1991. She holds a PhD on gender topics from the same university. She has also been running, together with her husband Carlos Gómez, the office gómez+álvarez arquitectes since 1992. Her main research fields are focused on architecture and urbanism with gender perspective. Her practice is centred on restoration and public buildings.

Carlos Gómez (*1965, Valencia, Spain)

has been Associate Professor at the Architectural Projects Department, Universitat Politècnica de València since 1992. He obtained his degree in architecture (with professional competences) at UPV in 1991. He holds a PhD on school buildings from the same university. He also runs, together with his wife Eva Álvarez, the office gómez+álvarez arquitectes since 1992. His research fields are focused on schools, daily life and photography. His practice is centred on restoration and public buildings.

Gesa Witthöft (*1964, Hamburg, Germany)

is a spatial planner. She has been researcher and lecturer at the Centre of Sociology within the Department of Spatial Planning at TU Wien in the subjects of Urban Renewal and Re-Development Planning, Social Aspects of Urban Planning and Architecture, Theory of Planning, Gender and Social Diversity, Participation and Communication in Planning Processes as well as Process Organisation since 2004. Her interdisciplinary education includes Geography, Pedagogics, German Studies as well as Sociology and Political Science. She worked as practitioner in socially oriented urban planning and teaches at other universities.

Petra Hirschler (*1972, Vienna, Austria)

is a lecturer and researcher at the Centre of Regional Planning and Regional Development within the Department of Spatial Planning at TU Wien. She completed her studies in urban and regional planning at the same academic institution. Before returning to her alma mater, Petra Hirschler spent 10 years working with a planning consultancy. Her research topics are gender mainstreaming, post carbon planning, renewable energy and mobility.

Aurélie Karlinger (*1989, Linz, Austria)
is student assistant at the Institute of Landscape Planning at BOKU Vienna. She currently studies landscape planning and landscape architecture at BOKU Vienna. In 2010/2011 she was a guest student at the Facoltà di Architettura dell'Università degli Studi di Firenze, Italy. Her current work emphases are the restructuring | redesign of public (open) space by investigating spatial practices with a focus on gender and diversity in planning.

Hannah-Katharina Jenal (*1986, Saarbrücken, Germany)
is an associate at the Research Center 'Energy and Environment' and studied urban planning at the Technical University of Vienna. Before she studied landscape architecture and environmental planning at Leibniz Universität Hannover, from where she went as an exchange student to the University of the West of England in 2009/2010. She works as associate editor of the magazine 'stadtform' in Vienna, which she had co-founded in 2014. Her research field is the urban night economy and the 24-city.

Anjoulie Brandner (*1986, Genalguacil, Spain)
currently studies landscape planning and landscape architecture at BOKU Vienna and works as a student assistant at the Institute of Landscape Planning. During her studies she promotes gender and diversity aspects in student politics. In her master's thesis she aims for understanding gender relations in land-use and livelihood strategies of small-scale farmers in the province of Malága (Andalusia, Spain).

Schriftenreihe „WEITER_DENKEN" des gender_archland (Forum für GenderKompetenz in Architektur Landschaft Plan,ung an der Leibniz Universität Hannover)

Publication series 'WEITER_DENKEN' (thinking_beyond) by gender_archland Forum for GenderCompetence in Architecture Landscape Planning at Leibniz Universität Hannover)

Band / Vol. 1 Beate Ahr, Roswitha Kirsch-Stracke: Die Naturschutz-Pionierinnen Margarete Boie (1880–1946) und Helene Varges (1877–1946) – Pilotstudie zur Quellen-lage. 2009.

Band / Vol. 2 Johanna Niescken, Lidewij Tummers: A different way to practise? Deutsche (Landschafts-) Architektinnen im internationalen Vergleich – A Transdisciplinary Project. 2011.

Band / Vol. 3 Ruth May, Barbara Zibell (Hg./eds.): GenderKompetenz in Architektur Landschaft Planung – Ideen Impulse Initiativen. 2012.

Band / Vol. 4 Ruth May: Migrantinnen als Existenzgründerinnen – Empirische Erhebungen in der Nordstadt von Hannover. 2014.

Band / Vol. 5 Barbara Zibell, Doris Damyanovic, Eva Álvarez (Hg./eds.): On Stage! Women in Landscape_Architecture and Planning. 2016.

Band / Vol. 6 Barbara Zibell, Maya Karacsony (Hg./eds.): Frauennetzwerke – heute morgen übermorgen? (Arbeitstitel). 2017.

https://www.gender-archland.uni-hannover.de/

Sponsoren | Sponsors

Wir danken der Leibniz Universitätsgesellschaft Hannover e. V. und der Landeshauptstadt Hannover, Referat für Frauen und Gleichstellung.

We thank the Leibniz Universitätsgesellschaft Hannover e. V. (university society association) and the City of Hanover, Department for Women and Equal Opportunities.